AN ASSESSMENT OF CHINA'S ANTI-SATELLITE AND SPACE WARFARE PROGRAMS, POLICIES AND DOCTRINES

Prepared for the U.S.-China Economic and Security Review Commission by Michael P. Pillsbury, Ph.D.

Report submitted to the Commission by the author on 19 January 2007

Table of Contents

EXECUTIVE SUMMARY

The first two parts of this study present the results of a survey of Chinese writings that discovered 30 proposals that China should acquire several types of anti satellite weapons. Many foreign observers have mistakenly claimed that China is a pacifistic nation and has no interest such weapons. The Director of the US National Reconnaissance Office Donald Kerr confirmed a Chinese laser had illuminated a US satellite in 2006. These skeptical observers dismissed that laser incident, but then appeared to be stunned by the reported Chinese destruction of a satellite January 11, 2007. China declined to confirm the event, but many foreign governments immediately protested,[1] including Japan, South Korea, Australia, Canada and Britain, while Russia's defense minister suggested the report may not be fully accurate.

A Chinese foreign ministry spokesman, while declining to confirm the incident, said other countries should not be alarmed. A US NSC spokesman said China fired a missile to destroy an orbiting weather satellite, making it the third country after the United States and the former Soviet Union to shoot down anything in space. If confirmed, the test would mean China could now theoretically shoot down spy satellites operated by other nations.

Parts 3 and 4 of this study recommend policy measures the US and other nations may consider. The ten measures are:

1. Possible US Countermeasures – Awareness, Assessing Damage, Forensics, Counter Strikes

Of the thirty Chinese proposals, one set would be particularly challenging to US military vulnerabilities in a crisis. In each of their books, Chinese Colonels Li, Jia and Yuan all advocated ***covert*** deployment of a sophisticated antisatellite weapon system to be used against United States in a surprise manner without warning. Even a small scale antisatellite attack in a crisis against 50 US satellites [assuming a mix of targeted military reconnaissance, navigation satellites, and communication satellites] could have a catastrophic effect not only on US military forces, but of the US civilian economy. It is not clear from US open sources how rapidly--if at all--United States could launch "spare" satellites to replace a few dozen that had been incapacitated in orbit by a Chinese attack. US sources refer to many [very expensive] countermeasures such as maneuvering satellites in orbit to escape destruction, using constellations of small satellites, rapid replacement with spares, and even prompt counter strikes on the Chinese launchers.[2]

A second set of Chinese concepts proposed in these open source writings would also be particularly challenging. Many of the concepts recommended include both jamming and attacking ground stations, rather than the permanent destruction of US satellites. In both cases, the Chinese authors imply the

---

[1] Hong Kong *AFP* January 19, 2007

[2] For a Unclassified list of countermeasures, see "Space Systems Survivability,." Uri Ra'anan and Robert L Pfaltzgraff, Jr, eds., *International Security Dimensions of Space*, Hamden CT, Archon Books, 1984, pp 87-93.

United States may lack the "forensic" ability to know which nation had neutralized US space systems through covert attack, jamming or destruction of ground stations by missile or Special Forces raids. The US Defense Department currently has put before Congress various proposals for enhancing situational awareness of space attack, but the ultimate approval of multiple-year funding is unknown.

2. Implications of Dialogues with These ASAT Authors

It is important that the US establish with the Chinese the serious importance to which we assign this published, detailed advocacy of Chinese weaponization of space. Access to ASAT specialists in China has been impossible in the DOD exchange programs in the past decade, according to some observers, because China prohibits ASAT experts from participating in the exchanges at all. The 3 NDU authors cited may never have visited the US, and, as started, seem unaware of the Congressional restraints on US space programs.

3. Detecting the Signatures of Future Chinese ASAT, impact of proposals on US policy decisions

An implication for the US intelligence community of these Chinese proposals would be the feasibility of identifying the developmental "signatures" of the recommended covert systems through normal intelligence collection. It may be difficult and probably impossible to detect the manufacturing and testing of many of the components that are proposed. The authors make clear in many of the recommendations that the acquisition of the systems and even their deployment are to be done covertly in a manner that cannot be detected by United States until the moment of their use by China in a crisis. Plasma attack, attacks on GPS, use of stealthy satellites, penetration and destruction of ground stations, jamming based on deceptive transmissions that imitate US signals, experimental units that can be converted in a crisis, ASATs fired from submarines -- all these concepts could potentially be concealed in advance of their use unless their signatures were anticipated. By definition, the Chinese government would deny the existence of such covert programs. Indeed, consideration must be given to the possibility that active duty colonels have been permitted to publish such proposals as an effort to influence US thinking regarding the potential vulnerabilities and lack of effectiveness of possible space based national missile defense components, thus discouraging their development and acquisition.

4. Concerns of Japan, India, European Union and Russia to Chinese ASAT

In terms of multilateral diplomacy and US alliances, one might ask whether other nations in addition to the United States have any concerns about these proposals and recommendations. The question would be whether China in the future may be the subject of pressure from the international community in addition to the United States.

5. Verification and On Site Inspections of an ASAT Agreement?

With respect to US arms control policy, some advocates such as Congressman Ed Markey have proposed that we re-think the question of refusal to negotiate or discuss the Chinese proposal to the UN conference on disarmament in Geneva on a non-verifiable agreement against weaponization in outer space. If such an agreement explicitly permitted American National missile defense and was verifiable with on-site inspection, it might merit negotiation. After all, China has accepted 100 visits by the inspection organization of the chemical weapons ban, so the precedent exists of China's accepting on-site inspections for international arms control agreements. Of course, the ban will be reciprocal so the United States would be compelled to accept inspections potentially of sensitive facilities under the control the national reconnaissance organization which manufactures highly classified US satellites and space systems.

6. Inference of Chinese Determinations of US Space Weapons activities and plans

With regard to future Sino-American exchanges and dialogue, one might ask what precisely are the catalysts or red lines that China seems to be suggesting will compel it to initiate the acquisition and deployment of space-based systems including antisatellite weapons. This issue is significant because an effort to engage China in a dialogue on space weapons would be futile and even naïve if the decision has already has been made by Chinese leaders because of their misperceptions of existing US policies and programs.

7. China's Proposed Space Weapons Ban and Current US Missile Defenses

In terms of understanding Chinese motives for a proposal in 2002 for a space weapons ban, that is, a decade after Chinese authors first recommended ASAT development, it is useful to keep in mind the relevant chronology. The American arms-control community has actively advocated a ban on space weapons systems since at least 1999, as can be seen in the appendix [Bibliography on Space Arms Control]. It seems possible therefore that China's proposal in Geneva in 2002 may have been stimulated by three or more years of observing US arms-control community proposals for space weapons bans.

If this hypothesis is correct, it helps to explain why China permitted the publication of three rather provocative books in 2001, 2002, and 2005 by military officers' with their proposals for covert deployment of antisatellite weapons directed at US assets. The publication of these books and other explicit recommendations advocating future antisatellite programs may have been authorized as part of a larger design to influence the US policy debate in the Congress and the media. One goal would be to oppose the extensive proposal by Senator Sam Nunn for a national missile defense system of 100 interceptors. If China essentially is threatening to deploy a robust ASAT system in the decade or two ahead, it makes a powerful case against even the current modest 20 interceptor system of in the present program.

8. Space-related Export Controls and Further Restrictions on Deemed Exports

There are substantial export control issues involved in any US decision to oppose or impede China's potential acquisition of antisatellite systems. We might ask whether more restrictive technology transfers on China could head off Chinese development of some or all of the antisatellite systems listed in the proposals identified in open sources. For example, nanotechnology laminated surfaces, miniature rocket motors; quick launch space vehicle propulsion, and directed energy technology (especially advance performance lasers), precision space guidance systems, and various bilateral technology exchanges such as the current program of the National Science Foundation for cooperation in remote sensing will become areas to examine for additional technology transfer restrictions. It would be a major project to identify and design new export controls on US technologies related to anti- satellite weapons acquisition and deployment.

9. PACOM and STRATCOM Role in Educating the PLA on Consequences of China's Use of ASAT

9. The US Department of Defense has extensive exchange programs in its "theater engagement plans" and may wish to play a greater role in deterring Chinese development of space weapons. Both Strategic Command and Pacific Command may wish to consider in their discussions on track one and track 1.5 whether to include information about the consequences of an attack on US military satellites in a crisis as part of their routine presentations on US defense policy and strategy to the Chinese.

10. China's Friends May Still Dismiss Chinese ASAT Ambitions For Lack of Evidence

It is difficult to rely on Chinese open source literature as the sole source for a persuasive strategic warning that vulnerable US military command, communications and sensitive national intelligence systems may all be in jeopardy in the decade ahead

If we know little about how space warfare may unfold because it has never happened, is it wise to dismiss the probative value of Chinese open source recommendations on the grounds that no one has yet seen China start to manufacture, test, exercise, and write doctrine for real space weapons? It would seem that open source materials containing recommendations for future ASAT concepts deserve more attention than to be completely dismissed, just as they cannot be considered to be completely definitive.

At a minimum, these writings suggest the need for a more assertive US engagement effort with the authors and their organizations. At a maximum, these writings suggest a major misperception by at least the authors and possible the Chinese leadership that US efforts to "weaponize space" are decades away, if the US Congress ever permits such efforts at all.

PART 1. OVERVIEW

Introduction

The US China Commission requested this survey of open source literature from the period 2003 through 2006 to identify internally generated Chinese perceptions, polices and proposals for possible programs related to antisatellite weapons and space warfare. The focus of this survey is the identification of specific internal Chinese proposals or recommendations regarding exploitation of US military vulnerabilities in space. The survey can be considered exhaustive and drew from all Chinese language material including Chinese professional military or aerospace technical journals and texts available through open source. Source books and articles were selected for attention in this survey if the source could be considered "mainstream" in development of Chinese policy and doctrine, and if they explicitly recommend that China should pursue one or more specific options or programs. Electronic searches of Chinese bibliographies by using terms like antisatellite weapon or space weapons generated hundreds of other "hits", but most of these items were purely descriptive of US and Russian programs and did not contain specific recommendations for future courses of action by China. Some common elements appear in several of the sourceworks cited here, indicating that these proposals and recommendations are representative of a consistent thread of policy development within China. Given the exhaustive scope of this survey, it is probably also a valid assumption that the authors cited here are principals in the discussions related to space warfare doctrine and development and are the primary proponents of the aggressive approaches which they advocate.

Twenty articles and three books published during the target period were selected as significant. From these books and articles, thirty specific recommendations for strategies or specific Chinese space weapons to employ against US vulnerabilities were identified and translated. Brief summaries of the thirty recommendations are provided below. Each is dealt with in detail in Part 2. The following conclusions may be made from this report:

- While China has publicly assumed a leadership position in international activities to ban space weapons, there is an active group within China not only advocating the weaponization of space but also putting forth specific proposals for implementation of a Chinese space based weapons program.
- The individuals authoring the source works cited herein represent the Chinese space war "hawk" group and may constitute the bulk of it, although the extent to which these proposals are being accepted sympathetically is not known.
- The recommendations cited in this report are courses of action being proposed publicly within China. Common threads of logic and approach, shared assumptions, use of similar expressions in key areas, and the scope of the work represented are indications of collusion among these individuals and possibly of organization.
- There may be covert activity in the development of space weaponry and space warfare plans which is not represented in open source literature, in fact the literature suggests that this might be so.
- Chinese development and deployment of systems and doctrines for space warfare may be partially in response to a perceived US threat, but US resistance to weaponization of space seems irrelevant in the articles cited.
- Chinese attitudes toward weaponization of space have been widely studied by the US, and several models have been proposed, based at least partially on consideration of some of the documents cited in this report. Other than common source material, these models share little and are even contradictory.
- There is an immediate opportunity for diplomatic action to forestall an inappropriate Chinese response to a perceived US threat and to engage elements of the Chinese policy forming community in productive and mutually beneficial confrontation.

- There are profound military preparedness implications associated with Chinese public advocacy of pre-emptive or deterrent attacks on specific US targets, both military and civilian, both independently and in support of theater combat operations.

This open source literature survey found no assertion that China currently possesses any type of ASAT weapons, or that the government of China has ordered the production of any such weapons. However, an unattributed interview in October 2006 at the Zhuhai air show that appeared in a Chinese owned newspaper bluntly stated China has such weapons now. This unusual article may be examined in the Documentary Appendix of this survey.

The books and journals selected in this survey support what earlier US authors have already concluded – that China is, at a minimum, interested in conceptual research on how to assess US vulnerabilities in space and how to destroy US satellites, but that China today possesses no such systems.

China has assumed a leadership position in proposing bans of spaced based weapons, so advocacy of future space based weapons systems by Chinese authors may be seen as a contradiction. While the likelihood of Chinese hypocrisy, deception, or merely lack of uniform policy implementation must be considered, an aggressive analysis of US space vulnerabilities and possibly even covert systems development by the Chinese may be considered consistent with a Chinese view that the weaponization of space by the US is inevitable, requiring a counterstrategy. The Documentary Appendix contains the full text of an unusually insightful article in a Hong Kong journal close to the PLA that explains this apparent contradiction in Chinese space policy. In 2002 China proposed a draft treaty to ban space weapons, but the US dismissed it as insufficient and unnecessary. The Hong Kong journal suggested that China will indeed have to develop and deploy space weapons to be ready as soon as [but apparently not before] the US proceeds with its own space weapons. The most recent US official position opposing the Chinese proposal is the August 2006 national space policy, and a more detailed speech by Under Secretary of State Robert Joseph December 12, 2006 that rejects the kind of agreement China proposed. [Joseph's speech is in the Documentary Appendix.] China has begun to characterize space testing by the US of some non-weapon systems as "space weapons," perhaps implying that China considers that the US has already crossed the line of the "inevitable" weaponization of space.

The US China Economic and Security Review Commission's 2006 report proposed a dialogue with China on space issues. The Report not only suggested that China may be developing the means to attack US space satellites, but also discussed a wide range of economic security issues including exports, jobs, and technology controls related to the US aerospace industry. The US media has been covering many of the economic security issues involved, such as the declining competitiveness of the US aerospace industry and whether hi tech export controls should be relaxed to permit NASA to cooperate with China in space exploration.

The China Commission recommended that "Congress direct the Administration to engage in a strategic dialogue with China on the importance of space surveillance, the military use of space, and space weapons. Such a dialogue should include strategic warning and verification measures." The Commission report also stated "China's military space doctrine is opaque, but some experts believe [emphasis added] that among the goals for the PLA's space program is obtaining space-related information dominance and the ability to disable its opponents' space assets in order to disrupt their space-based information and navigation systems in the event of conflict…. With regard to the second space objective, there is evidence suggesting that China ''is developing the capacity to deny . . . [the use of space] to others . . . [and has] at least one ground-based laser anti-satellite research and development program underway[emphasis added]."

This study will present Chinese proposals published in the last few years to attack US space satellites and to use space weapons to defeat US military forces. When considering these Chinese concepts of future space warfare, it is important to appreciate that the Chinese state their civilian space program and their civilian economy will be the foundation for space warfare. This linkage between civilian and military space development programs places the issue in the context of economic security as well as military security. In 2001, Congress created a 12 member Commission which recommended attention to aerospace, but a GAO study in 2006 reported limited progress. There is a major workforce crisis in the aerospace industry.3 Over 600,000 scientific and technical aerospace jobs have been lost since 1998, and these losses, coupled with pending retirements, represent a loss of skill, experience, and intellectual capital to the industry. The positive impact of the aerospace industry on the U.S. economy is significant, with the industry estimating $170 billion in sales and approximately 625,000 people employed in 2005.5 The importance of this industry to the U.S. economy will continue to grow in the future. The U.S. aerospace industry consistently shows a foreign trade surplus—reaching $31 billion in 2004. Aerospace exports constituted 6.9 percent of the total value of U.S.-exported merchandise in 2004. It provides the foundation for US military space activities. The federal government is involved in many aspects of aerospace, such as national security, space exploration, and related R&D. NASA and Defense are major federal agencies most significantly involved in aerospace activities. Trends in aerospace R&D are described in an appendix 6.

All of the recommendations cited here are oriented to the future, some as far ahead as 2025, and thus are consistent with the putative position that China will never be the first to weaponize space. Chinese authors appear generally to assume that the US, on the other hand, is intent on weaponizing space. Interestingly, these authors universally fail to acknowledge the consistenetly successful struggle of the arms control-minded members of the US Congress to block funding for space weapons during the past decade or more.

If the recommendation of the USCC for a strategic dialogue with China on space is accepted by Congress and the President, such a dialogue may be profitably supplemented with an exchange program that would include the authors of these thirty proposals to encourage them to modify their perceptions of that the US intends to deploy space weapons. The documentary appendix to this report contains two articles with interviews of the US Air Force that make clear space weapons are at least two decades away from deployment, even in the unlikely event that the US Congress permits funding. The US may be placed in an awkward position if China procedes with an aggressive policy toward space weaponization while the US remains passive. Equally undesirable may be an expensive and counterproductive space weapons race. Open dialogue, active understanding of respective positions and progress toward treaty based bans on specific verifiable space related activities may be the most expedient course.

The summary below provides each of the thirty numbered recommendations in direct quotation. Key words of each proposal are placed in boldface type for clarity. Part 2 provides longer exerpts and details. Appendices provide details on source documents, a larger bibliography on Chinese space related literature, listings of comparable non-Chinese sources of weaponization of space, and related non-Chinese articles

Summary of Chinese Recommendations on Space Weaponization

1.   Basic space combat capability

---

3 Source: GAO Report to the Ranking Democratic Member, Subcommittee on Aviation, Committee on Transportation and Infrastructure, House of Representatives, "U.S. Aerospace Industry Progress in Implementing Aerospace Commission Recommendations, and Remaining Challenges" September 2006, GAO-06-920.

2. **Destroy or temporarily incapacitate all enemy space vehicles above our territory**
3. **Civil-use technology that can also be used in military applications**
4. **Land-based anti-satellite weapons and anti-satellite satellites**
5. **A space experimental unit and a national research and command center**
6. **Counter United States' missile defense systems**
7. **"Assassin's mace" weapons (shashoujian) with space attack capability**
8. **Construction should be carried out secretly**
9. **"Assassin's mace" space weapons**
10. **Develop space for combat support**
11. **Maintain our good international image [by covert development]**
12. **Space strike weapons concealed and launched only in crisis**
13. **Missiles [which] require less launch preparation time**
14. **Emergency/crisis launch units**
15. **Formulation of precise emergency/crisis launch plans**
16. **Surprise attacks in space [and] on information sources, command and control centers, communication hubs, including use of ground troops**
17. **Sea-based anti-satellite platform**
18. **Submarine launched Chinese ASATs**
19. **Attack GPS with anti-satellite satellites**
20. **Attack GPS with high energy laser weapons**
21. **Attack GPS with high altitude weather monitoring rockets**
22. **attack [GPS ground] stations using missles or troops**
23. **Orbital ballistic missiles**
24. **Plasma Attack against Low-Orbit Spy Satellites**
25. **Stealth satellites**
26. **Reconnaissance systems that resist jamming**
27. **Jamming [to] disable US command and control in wartime**
28. **Kinetic Kill Vehicles**
29. **Satellite Attacks on Earth Targets**
30. **Directed Energy or beam weapons**

NDU Book 2001 - Space War

Colonel Li Daguang in his book *Space War* published by NDU in 2001 makes at least 8 proposals, which are echoed to some extent in two other NDU Press books by Colonel Yuan and Colonel Jia which each offer an additional 3 recommendations on future space weapons. .

1. "The planning of space weapons development can be divided into two stages with the first stage covering from now until 2010. In the first stage **we must strive to make our space weapon systems possess support and safeguard capabilities as well as basic space combat capability**....They should also have a certain combat capability in space, particularly in regards to defensive capability."

2. "In the second stage, we should build on the foundation of the first stage by further improving our offensive and defensive capability of space weapon systems. In particular, **the offense capability in space should, if necessary, be capable of destroying or temporarily incapacitating all enemy space vehicles that fly in space above our sovereign territory.**"

3. "We should combine military and civilian technology and integrate peacetime and wartime facilities. Space equipment is costly to develop and maintain, **so it is important to have civil-use technology that can also be used in military applications.**"

4. "In the near term, **the key developments should be anti-satellites weapons including land-based anti-satellite weapons and anti-satellite satellites.**"

5. "**A space experimental unit and a national research and command center must be established.**"

6. "When needed, this experimental center could be turned into a military space operational command center or the highest command headquarters. Specifically, **these organizations should focus on countering the United States' missile defense systems as well as countermeasures related to the integration of Taiwan into these systems.**"

7. "In addition, to meet the requirements of defeating the United States in a war over Taiwan; the **PLA should have "assassin's mace" weapons (shashoujian) with space attack capability.**"

8. "Considering certain constraints from the international society, **the construction of such a unit [for space weapons experiments] should be carried out secretly** by keeping a low profile."

NDU Book 2002 - On Space Operations

Colonel Jia Junming echoes many themes found in Li Daguang's earlier book Space War. Space War and Space Operations are in turn consistent with the bolder proposals in the third book, Integrated Space Campaigns.

9. Jia advocates **space weapons for China**, calling them "assassin's maces."

10. Jia recommends a two phased approach: "For our country, in phase one, 2000-2015, **we must develop space for combat support.** In phase two, 2015 to 2030, then **develop "limited space deterrence and "assassin's mace" space weapons.**"

11. Covertness – "**[Our future space weapons program] should be low profile and 'intense internally but relaxed in external appearance** [nei jin wai song]" to maintain our good international image and position "

NDU Book 2005 - Joint Space War Campaigns

12. Colonel Yuan Zelu, proposes **an orbiting network of space strike weapons which will be concealed and launched only in a crisis or "emergency' in order to deter the US with limited attacks on US space assets** in order to "bring the opponent to his knees" and to deter US actions. Yuan writes "Space-based attack networks are made up of the network systems of the various strike platforms that are in orbit. International space law prohibits this kind of weaponry deployment and even though space-based directed energy weapons and space-based kinetic energy weapons and other space-based weapons are successfully going through research and development, they still cannot be rapidly deployed in orbit. "

13.. "For these reasons, emergency/crisis launchers to organize the network will become the necessary option for constructing a space-based strike network in wartime. First, one must **research, develop, and test equipment for new types of astronautic carrier vehicles… and require less launch preparation time in order to greatly reduce launch preparation times and increase the rapid reaction capabilities of space launch units and flight units.**

14. Second, **emergency/crisis launch units must be set up**.

15. Third, **complete war preparation [warning] systems should be established**… to guarantee that on the day that it receives launch orders it will immediately be able to launch space-based fire platforms into orbit and complete its networking tasks in the shortest amount of time. Fourth, **scientific and precise emergency/crisis launch plans must be formulated.**"

16. **Surprise attacks in space for huge psychological impact on the opponent's policymakers.**" In future military struggles, space shock and awe strikes will occur when other means of space deterrence have proven ineffective and will be the final step made in order to achieve the goal of deterrence. If a space shock and awe strike is still ineffective, then it means that space deterrence activities should be wholly abandoned. For these reasons, the execution of space shock and awe **strikes must involve the prudent use of troops**, thorough command, and strict control in order for them to bring an opponent to its knees through a combination of deterrence and combat.

Therefore, when space army commanders are organizing and commanding space shock and awe strike activities, they should focus on mastering the following four points:

First, the painstaking selection of strike objectives. The goal of a space shock and awe strike is still to deter the enemy, not to provoke the enemy into combat. For this reason, the objectives selected for strike must be few and precise. Points of support and key points within an enemy's operational system of organization should be selected. For example, **strikes should be carried out on important information sources, command and control centers, communication hubs, and other objectives**. This will shake the structure of the opponent's operational system of organization and will create a huge psychological impact on the opponent's policymakers."

Exerpts from Journals and Articles

17. Professor Liu Huanyu of the Dalian Naval Academy: advocates "Sea-Based Anti-Satellite Platforms"

"China is in urgent need of new effective defense forces. Constrained by its national resources, the broad goals of economic development, and the international environment in the area, it is impossible and unnecessary for China to develop large scale aircraft carriers…..What China needs now is an effective capability to intervene on the ocean, which means a new sea power. The **sea-based anti-satellite platform is a major component of the new sea power and must be given a high priority**. If this new avenue is explored as soon as possible, China can hopefully improve its sea power dramatically within 10 years

18. Liu recommends that **submarine launched Chinese ASATs** may be superior to surface ships.

Chen Xuejun and Lang Daqiang in their "Methods for Defeating GPS" ask "So what is the Achilles heel of GPS? And reply "An analysis of the working principles of GPS reveals three major weaknesses.

19. **Attack GPS with anti-satellite satellites** – several options.

20. **Attack GPS with high energy laser weapons** – several options.

21. **Attack GPS with high altitude weather monitoring rocket** – the space pellets option.

22. A GPS system cannot position or navigate without a ground control system. Once the ground control is damaged, it would no longer be able to accurately guide or navigate long range weapons. Therefore, **submarine launched missiles or long range weapons can be used to attack these [GPS ground] stations, or the Special Forces may be trained to effectively infiltrate and destroy the stations**.

23. Zhao Ruian advocates orbital ballistic missiles, "a new-concept strategic ballistic missile is a multi-task, multi-role attack weapon capable of implementing random orbit transfer from earth orbits and can serve the function of an intercontinental ballistic missile, an anti-satellite weapon, and an orbital bomber weapon. For China's national security, it is undoubtedly important to study the development status of space weapons in the world and to **investigate the ideas and related technologies of orbital ballistic missiles.**"

24. **Plasma Attack against Low-Orbit Spy Satellites** is Feasible [2005][4]
This article addresses "the effectiveness of using plasma to disrupt low-orbit reconnaissance satellite operations and proposes a scheme for using plasma against satellites. Analysis of satellite charging and discharging effects and mechanisms in a plasma environment indicates that plasma damages low-orbit satellites

25. "There is a great deal of work to do to **develop a stealth satellite**. In this paper, the optical signatures of a satellite and its stealth related issues were preliminarily explored. A number of schemes were proposed. The rationality and feasibility of these schemes need to be jointly investigated with relevant experts." [5]

26. Space Electronic Jamming [2006]."**Reconnaissance systems must also be able to counter jamming and release effective jamming**. Otherwise, the space-based reconnaissance system does not possess survivability in a modern warfare environment. "

---

[4] Author is an assistant professor at the College of Astronautics, Northwestern Polytechnic University, and holds a Doctorate in plasma applications.

[5] Li Yubo,(Institute of Electronic Engineering, Hefei, Anhui 230037, ChinaLi Yubo is a lecturer at the Institute of Electronic Engineering, engaged in research on computer and optoelectronic detection.

27 Six Studies on Jamming US Classified Data Links [JTIDS] suggest a clear focus on **disabling US command and control in wartime.** Authors are from Electronic Warfare Institute, Xian Electronic Science and Technology University, Xian, the School of Telecommunication Engineering, Xian University, Department of Electronics and Information Engineering, HUST, the Electronic Engineering Institute of the PLA (Hefei),

28. Ten Studies of how to **develop Kinetic Kill Vehicles** by technical authors from the School of Automation, Beijing University of Aviation and Aerospace; Harbin Institute of Technology; Second Research Academy of China Aerospace Science & Industry Corporation [CASIC] Academy of Equipment Command & Technology, Beijing Aerospace Automatic Control Institute, and the Northeastern Polytechnic University, College of Astronautics.

29. **Satellite Attacks on Earth Targets** [2005]. The greatest advantage of a space-based ground attack weapon system is its high speed and short reentry time. It is extremely difficult for the enemy to intercept such a weapon. It requires a more powerful high performance computer on board. In order to minimize the initial error, it is preferable to launch the war capsule at a larger angle of reentry. The guidance algorithm will produce a better effect and the point of impact will be more accurate.

30. Research on Beam Weapons Proposals. Since at least 1995, more than 20 authors have detailed their research on **Directed Energy or beam weapons as part of a larger class of weapons known to the Chinese as "new concept weapons"** (xin gainian wuqi), which include high power lasers, high power microwaves, railguns, and particle beam weapons. Most authors are affiliated with five institutes: Shanghai Institute of Optics and Fine Mechanics (lasers; adaptive optics);Anhui Institute of Optics and Fine Mechanics (adaptive optics);Institute of Optoelectronics (adaptive optics); Dalian Institute of Chemistry and Physics (lasers); China Academy of Engineering Physics (CAEP) and the Northwest Nuclear Weapons Research and Design Academy) which has developed and tested China's nuclear warheads.

Current US Views on China's ASAT Policy

A wide range of views exists among US scholars about China's possible intentions and capabilities with respect to space weapons and ASATs, which is understandable in light of the limited evidence available from open sources. This survey of Chinese open sources and the identification of thirty recommendations may assist in resolving some of these differences, but only much greater Chinese transparency would resolve them all.

One point on which everyone appears to agree is that the US military is extremely vulnerable in space and should develop plans for defense of its space assets.[6] Everyone appears to disagree on the precise goals, pace, current capabilities and relationship between Chinese arms control proposals and their publicly stated R&D programs. Most agree that the US is highly vulnerable for over a decade. In 1996, Gen Thomas S. Moorman, USAF, former Vice CSAF and commander, Air Force Space Command, stated, "Desert Storm . . . was a watershed event in military space applications because for the first time, space systems were both integral to the conflict and critical to the outcome of the war.[7]

1. An early study by Mark Stokes in 1999 concluded that the open source literature "does not provide any clear indication that the Central Military Commission has directed the defense industrial complex to move toward ASAT testing or production stages. Technical writings do, however, clearly point to conceptual assessments on various ASAT systems and related technologies."

No author has challenged Stokes' conclusion, but there is a range of American opinions on closely related issues of China's plans and capabilities to deploy space weapons.

2. According to Ioannis Koskinas, China recognizes U.S. dependence on space assets and is bolstering its counterspace capabilities. He cites the DOD's 2004 report on Chinese military capabilities, stating "the PRC realizes that the US is so dependent on space and, thus, it remains interested in counterspace capabilities that can deny or degrade America's ability to react to a PRC-Taiwan conflict." [8]

3. Theresa Hitchens sees China reacting to the US in pursuing space weapons to counter American space dominance:

"....[M]uch of China's interest in space seems to stem directly from concerns about

---

[6] Gen. Lance Lord, Commander, Air Force Space Command, quoted in Louis Arane-Barradas, "Civilian Sector the Biggest Space Customer," *Academy Spirit*, 24 February 2006.

[7] ." AFDD 4, *Space Operations Doctrine*, 10 July 1996, http://www.fas.org/spp/military/docops/usaf/afdd4.htm. "During the 1991 Persian Gulf War . . . over 60 military satellites and others from the commercial and civil sectors were employed." George W. Bradley III, "A Brief History of the Air Force in Space," *High Frontier: The Journal for Space and Missile Professionals* 2, no. 2 (Fall 2004): 7. Between 1995 and 2005, over 75 Air University research papers, articles, and books were produced dealing with space issues, and significant DOD service doctrine has been approved, including AFDD 2-2, *Space Operations*; AFDD 2-2.1, *Counterspace Operations*; AFDD 4, *Space Operations Doctrine*; JP 3-14, *Space Operations*; Army Field Manual (FM) 100-18, *Space Support to Army Operations*; and *National Security Space (NSS) Acquisition Policy* 03-01. *United States Space Command Long-Range Plan: Implementing USSPACECOM Vision for 2020* (Peterson AFB, CO: US Space Command, Director of Plans, April 1998), 4–5; *Report of the Commission to Assess United States National Security Space Management and Organization* (Washington, DC: Space Commission, 2001), 18, http://www.defenselink.mil/pubs/space20010111.pdf; Col James E. Haywood, USAF, "Making Vision a Reality: Delivering Counterspace Capability to the High Frontier," *High Frontier: The Journal for Space and Missile Professionals* 2, no. 2 (Fall 2004): 54.

[8] Ioannis Koskinas, "Space Warfare Foolosophy: Should the United States be the First Country to Weaponize Space?." *Air & Space Power Journal*, January 2005.

American military activities in space. According to the Nuclear Threat Initiative, China's worries about protecting its space-based assets are due to concern about American development of missile defenses and future American global dominance as a result of American space power." [9]

4. Yoshihara and Martel argue that China views space power as the key to economic modernization.

"China's obsession with national prestige, which forms the backdrop for its commercial and military interests, also animates the country's space policy. The PRC government has long boasted about its status as one of the few major space-faring nations." [10]

5. Robert Antonellis and William Murray conclude China's space program is driven by a desire for national prestige:

"Beijing views U.S. military power in the Pacific as an impediment to China's aspiration of becoming the dominant regional power. Beijing is modernizing and expanding China's military capabilities not only to keep an increasingly independent Taiwan in line, but also to effectively deny the U.S. military the ability to operate against China or its interests in Asia. Chinese military planners have realized that area denial operations require the conduct of space-based surveillance and the other dual-use benefits of space technology. The Dragon is eyeing the moon because the Dragon is also eyeing us." [11]

6. China could provide space services to adversaries of the U.S., according to David Thompson:

"However, without global land, sea, or air capabilities, the military impact of China's space programs is likely to be limited to defense of China's homeland and support of regional activities undoubtedly pointed at Taiwan, the Spratly Islands, Tibet, and other areas of similar proximity and sensitivity to China. In a conflict, China also could assist nations allied against the US by providing launch support, ASAT activities, ISR data, and similar services." [12]

David Thompson also suggests that China views space power as the key to counter U.S. strength:

"For example, in 2000 the PRC Defense Minister said that space-power is viewed as the key to China's planning to supplant the United States. PLA doctrine would deny the advantages of space to the US, seeking to leverage space for China's own advantage." [13]

7. Colonel Clayton Chun identifies the concern that China may be willing to sell its space technology to US adversaries:

[9] Theresa Hitchens. "Monsters and Shadows: Left Unchecked, American Fears Regarding Threats to Space Assets Will Drive Weaponization." Disarmament Forum. 2003, p. 18.
[10] Yoshihara, Toshi and William C. Martel. " Averting a Sino-U.S. Space Race," Washington Quarterly. Autumn 2003.
[11] Antonellis, Robert and William S. Murray. "China's Space Program: The Dragon Eyes the Moon (and Us)." Orbis. Fall 2003, pp. 645-652.
[12] David J. Thompson, . China in Space: Civillian and Military Developments. Maxwell AFB, AL: USAF Air University, August 2001.
[13] David J. Thompson, China in Space: Civilian and Military Developments, Maxwell AFB, AL: USAF Air University, August 2001.

"China's threat as a space power goes beyond its own capabilities. The Chinese export their technology, selling their ballistic missile assets and space launch capabilities." [14]

8. According to Steven Lambakis, a 1994 U.S. Navy war game showed that China could devastate the US by attacking our space assets

"Some instruction on these points may be found in a simulated war against the People's Republic of China conducted at the Naval War College in the spring of 1994. The war game, set in the year 2010, was a part of the Pentagon's ongoing study of the revolution in military affairs. In the scenario, Beijing provokes the U.S. Navy into patrolling China's shores, luring vulnerable aircraft carriers and other surface ships within range of precision-guided cruise missiles. The Chinese begin their ambush by attacking U.S. satellites, which confounds American targeting abilities and precludes any significant counter-offensive by the U.S. Navy. The Chinese also use space-based assets to enhance the effectiveness of their own forces. U.S. players in this war game were routed, their forces hit before they could throw up adequate defenses." [15]

9. France and Adams believe that China is developing space power capabilities to counter U.S. conventional strength, not as a response to U.S. space weapons.

"Contrary to the views of space sanctuary and space arms control advocates, fear of an emerging US capability to destroy Chinese satellites is not the primary catalyst behind Beijing's counterspace moves. Chinese interests in space weapons do not hinge on winning a potential US-Chinese ASAT battle or participating in a space arms race. Two other motivations play a much greater role in cultivating China's desire for counterspace weapons: to counter the space-enabled advantage of US conventional forces; and to guarantee the viability of Chinese nuclear forces in the face of emerging American missile defenses." [16]

France and Adams assert that China already possesses both the intent and "growing capability" to threaten U.S. space assets:

"China possesses both the intent and a growing capability to threaten US space systems in the event of a future clash between the two countries. The PLA's development of ASAT weapons is primarily not a reaction to US space control initiatives. It is driven instead by very practical considerations of regional security and influence, and the desire to conduct asymmetric warfare against a superior foe if conflict arises. First, Beijing seeks to offset the dominance of US conventional forces by exploiting their dependence on space borne information assets. Second, China hopes to guarantee the viability of its nuclear deterrent by holding the critical space-segment of American missile defense systems at risk. Both of these goals are deeply rooted in the issue of Taiwanese reunification and the potential for armed conflict over the status of the island. China's growing capability to attack American satellites could play an important role in a future military confrontation over Taiwan." [17]

---

[14] Clayton K. S.Chun, Shooting Down a Star: Program 437, the U.S. Nuclear ASAT System and Present Day Copycat Killers. Maxwell AFB, AL: USAF Air University, April 2000.

[15] Steven Lambakis, "Space Control in Desert Storm and Beyond," *Orbis*, Summer 1995.

[16] Martin E.B. France and Richard J. Adams. "The Chinese Threat to US Superiority." *High Frontier Journal*, Winter 2005, p. 18.

[17] Ibid., p. 21.

10 Many authors note that China appears to have enjoyed remarkable cooperation and technical assistance in its civil space program from Russia, France and Germany, but no one details its role in China's progress.[18] China's own *Space Activities Report in 2006* cites remarkable progress with many partners.

11. Kevin Pollpeter notes in a Rand Study that Chinese authors all state that the weaponization of space is "inevitable." This is significant as a catalyst for China's stated "defensive" interest in developing future space weapons. Pollpeter cites passages from Li Daguang's *Space War* extensively.[19]

12. One of the strongest assertions is the study by Philip Saunders and colleagues in 2002. Their views are significant and well worth excerpting at length:

"A number of analysts, including some in the U.S. defense and intelligence communities, believe that China has the technical capacity to rapidly develop effective counter-space capabilities. However, China's technical ability to develop and deploy advanced space weapons such as ASATs is uncertain.…China still lacks a number of capabilities that would be required for a viable ASAT program. …Although open source information clearly indicates Chinese interest and scientific research in ASAT weapons and technologies, the available evidence is insufficient to determine if China has an active program to develop and deploy ASAT weapons. …. Although the Chinese have a strong strategic motivation to pursue asymmetric programs such as ASAT weapons, serious questions remain about their technical capabilities and political will to undertake such a costly program. China has been extremely vocal in international fora with regards to the demilitarization of outer space and is a strong proponent of a multilateral treaty banning space weapons, indicating internal pressures may exist that could slow progress towards ASAT development and deployment. This seems to signal that Beijing, although interested for strategic reasons in counter-space and ASAT capabilities, is not keen to enter an expensive and potentially open-ended space race. Given China's limited space capabilities and stated interest in preventing an arms race in outer space, Beijing's ultimate commitment to developing ASAT weapons remains ambiguous."

Present Level of Development and Deployment of Chinese ASAT Capability

One important question is whether there is a covert ASAT program today as part of a secret plan to develop space weapons. Such a program would not be revealed in this survey of open source material, and in fact the proposals translated in part 2 could be construed as "cover" for such a current program, or the authors are simply not aware of such a hypothetical current clandestine ASAT program. Three recent Chinese denials in 2006 merit our close attention.

China Denies Developing Anti-Satellite Laser [2006]

We quote in full an article by a reporter in the US, Zhong Xiang: "China Says South Pole Radar Station Only For Scientific Studies but US Military 'Worried'"[20]

---

[18] Andrey Kirillov, "China to Buy Russian Equipment for Manned Space Missions," Itar-Tass, March 14, 1995, in FBIS-SOV-95-049; "Paris, Beijing Discuss Strategic Space Partnership," Les Echos, January 29, 1997, p. 11, in FBIS-CHI-97-020; Liu Jiyuan, "Strengthening Space Cooperation, Looking Forward to the 21st Century," Zhongguo Hangtian, June 1996, pp. 7-8, in FBIS-CST-96-015; Zhongguo Hangtian Kaizhan Quanfangwei Guoji Hezuo, (China Space Opens Comprehensive International Cooperation Meeting), Zhongguo Hangtian Bao, October 3, 1994, p. 1.

[19] Monterey Institute of International Studies, 2002.

[20] Beijing Xinhua Wang WWW-Text in Chinese 07 Feb 06.

"China is attempting to set up a high frequency radar station at the South Pole Zhongshan Station, to be used to probe and research the space environment of the polar region. Yet this purely scientific project has attracted the "attention and concern" of the US military. A February 2 report in the US publication, World Tribune states experts within the US military worry this effort by China is to "sabotage US spy satellites." In the article entitled "China Radar at South Pole Could Sabotage US Satellites," the World Tribune gave a description which bordered on outright fabrication. According to the analysis of US security specialists, China's establishing a high frequency radar station at the distant South Pole is for military aims. Because US reconnaissance satellites pass over South Pole air space several times, if the radar emits an anti-spy light beam, it could jam or sabotage them. Last year, the Defense Department's report on China's military strength pointed out that China is presently researching and building an anti-satellite system (ASAT). Although China has officially stated its high frequency radar station will be used for the observation of the spatial environment of the South Pole, in the eyes of US military specialists China's space plans are all connected with military applications. Responding to the censure of the United States, Chinese military experts say China's establishing a high frequency radar station at the South Pole will be used for scientific research. Its power will be very low, and its influence on the ionosphere very small. Additionally, the United States, England, and South Africa all have similar radar installations at the South Pole. It is "preposterous in the extreme" to link China's radar installation with the sabotage of US spy satellites and the so-called Chinese "anti-satellite plan."

A second article denies the recent laser attack story:[21]

"The US military journal, *Defense News*, says in an article it published on its website the other day that China attempted to use high-energy laser to interfere with US satellites flying over China's airspace and "blind" them. The fact is that China is pursuing the policy of using the space peacefully at a time when many other countries are scrambling for space supremacy; and that the United States' exaggeration of China's counter-satellite technology is only an attempt to seek an excuse to justify its development of space weapons.

"US Vilifies China for Using Laser To Blind US Satellites

"In the article, "China Attempts To Blind US Satellites with Laser," the author cited an anonymous source as saying that over the past several years China tried to use high-energy land-based laser many times to test the ways to blind US satellites whenever they flew over China's airspace. The article adds that it was unclear how many times China has conducted these tests and whether the tests were successful.

"The fact is that the information about China using laser to blind US satellites is entirely a conjecture. Because of China's policy of using the space peacefully, China is against militarization of the space. Besides, striking satellites with laser is a high-tech undertaking that requires enormous investments. Moreover, attacking another country's satellites certainly will trigger international disputes. Thus, there are many factors -- policy, capital, technology and diplomatic -- that constrain China's development of this capability. The truthfulness of the information is therefore questionable. However, when we look at the situation of the United States, its dedication to seizing space supremacy and extending the battleground to the space is an indisputable fact. According to the latest databank of satellites that the US "Union of Concerned Scientists" has made public, the United States has 413 of the 811 assorted satellites now

---

[21] Zhang Mingqi: "Tactics for Handling Satellites,"Beijing *Huanqiu Shibao* 28 Sep 2006 p 8.

circling the earth -- or over half of all the satellites. In addition to launching satellites from time to time, the United States has also been studying the development of anti-satellite weapons. In recent years it has come up with the policies and the budgets for building a "military sky force," regarding satellite offense and defense as vital capabilities that US armed forces must possess in the future. ….

"Countries Are Scrambling for Developing AntiSatellite Weapons

"Many countries in the world are now developing their anti-satellite weapons. The "Transformation Flight Plans" [zhuan xing fei xing ji hua] that the US Armed Forces made public in January 2005 listed all the key projects for future space weapons, such as land-based laser anti-satellite weapons, air-launched anti-satellite missiles, and air-based directed energy weapons. Russia is also not far behind. It has developed the concept of anti-satellite weapons long time ago and has been hard at work in studying the development of new conceptual weapons.

"All these anti-satellite weapons are still at the research/development and testing stage. These weapons have yet to be deployed in the space. However, as we can observe from the trend in the United States, the Bush Administration is ready to promulgate a new national space policy to pave the legal way for deploying weapons in the space. *Once the United States begins to follow this path, militarization of the space will be inevitable.* By that time mankind's dream of using the space peacefully will be shattered and the space will inevitably become another killing field of mankind [Emphasis added]. "

Part 2. Thirty Chinese Recommendations for Space Weapons

Covert Space Weapons

- NDU Book 1 on Space War – Covert Space Weapons [2001]

Space Warfare is written by a professor at the PLA's NDU who received a bachelor's degree in engineering from the PLA Zhengzhou Mapping Institute in 1983 and a master's degree in strategic studies from NDU in 1998. He teaches courses on military technology and equipment. Colonel Li appears to call on the Air Force not the Second Artillery to take the lead in space warfare.

> Since its establishment 50 years ago, our Air Force has gained tremendous achievement in its modernization process. However, our Air Force modernization drive and development lags behind the world military trend. It is important to acknowledge this. We need to establish in the Air Force the notion of controlling air and space.[22]

Meeting the challenges of space warfare requires the development of new technology. The author continues:

> Based on the needs of national security and our nation's space development, the planning of space weapons development can be divided into two stages with the first stage covering from now until 2010. In the first stage we must strive to make our space weapon systems possess support and safeguard capabilities as well as basic space combat capability. In addition, they can complement our operations on the ground, sea and air and at the same time provide effective surveillance, monitoring, early warning, communications, navigation, and positioning support to our combat units. They should also have a certain combat capability in space, particularly in regards to defensive capability. [p. 415]

> Colonel Li advocates that China should wait until the second stage [2010-2025] for the really important preparations:

> In the second stage, we should build on the foundation of the first stage by further improving our offensive and defensive capability of space weapon systems. In particular, the offense capability in space should, if necessary, be capable of destroying or temporarily incapacitating all enemy space vehicles that fly in space above our sovereign territory. [p 415]

The author then gives a five-step plan for developing the nation's space warfare ability, one key part on which depends on obtaining foreign cooperation.

"Fifth, combine military and civilian technology and integrate peacetime and wartime facilities. As space equipment is costly to develop and maintain, it is important to have civil-use technology that can also

---

[22] Pp 409-410 Li Daguang, *Space Warfare*, Beijing NDU Press, 2001 A copy of this book is on file at the USCC.

be used in military applications. The dual use nature of space technology allows space development to adapt to the military-civilian compatible model of development. Therefore, the development of space technology must serve military missions as well as national economic development.

Colonel Li Recommends an Experimental Space Force Unit

"In addition to technology development, the PLA must change its internal structure to better meet the challenges of space warfare. A space testing unit and a national research and command center must be established. These will be the organizational and leading bodies of China's future space operations that will be responsible for the uniform coordination of command and control of all forces related to the building of space forces. Its main mission should consist of three aspects.

First, to guide the strategy for developing space operations by planning and coordinating the development of space technology and to organize and guide the research and study of space warfare theories as well as top level design and system building.

Second, these organizations will lead and organize the development of space weapon systems. They will also study how to adapt current space technology to military applications and plan and coordinate the preparations for building a future space unit.

Third, they will be in charge of studying the military application of China's current military space forces and its training and management, which includes the uniform management and maintenance of current space weapon systems. When needed this center could be turned into a military space operational command center or the highest command headquarters.
Specifically, these organizations should focus on countering the United States' missile defense systems as well as countermeasures related to the integration of Taiwan into these systems. [Emphasis added.]

Assassin's Mace

 In addition, to meet the requirements of defeating the United States in a war over Taiwan; the PLA is urged to possess weapons that can act as "assassins maces" (shashoujian) with space attack capability. Therefore, China must construct a small, yet elite space operational testing unit as soon as possible. The goal and purpose of forming this unit is to explore, assess and implement space warfare concepts and to accumulate experience to implement space deterrent and operational capabilities. This will also act as the foundation of a future space unit….".

     Colonel Li writes that considering international opposition to the weaponization of space, the construction of a space force should be carried out **covertly**:

> Military space force development and application is a complex project involving a multitude of units inside and outside the military that has a high degree of difficulty and a long development span with the necessity for a high degree of command and control as well as a high degree of sensitivity. Considering certain constraints from the international society, the construction of such a unit should be carried out secretly by keeping a low profile. We should also use our military's current space equipment and institutions and avoid large-scale institutional change to maximize the effect by using the least investment.

     He continues:

We must understand the situation of our space force construction and focus on the possible space operational issues when resolving the Taiwan problem. Studying and developing operational models and campaign methods of real operational significance with a special focus on those that can effectively contain Air Force support for Taiwan by the United States. Judging from our country's current space technology level and situation, we should focus on studying future space terrestrial

Space Operations

- NDU Book 2 on Space Operations [2002]

Colonel Jia Junming echoes many themes found in Li Daguang's earlier book *Space War*. *Space War* and *Space Operations* [23] are in turn consistent with the bolder proposals in the third book, *Integrated Space Campaigns*. On page 140 of *Space Operations*, Colonel Jia advocates "limited" space weapons for "deterrence" and calls them "assassin's maces." For "our country," he suggests that in phase one [2000-2015] China develop space for combat support and later in phase two [2015 to 2030] [p152] China should develop "limited space deterrence" assassin's mace weapons.

His recommendations parallel those of Colonel Li on the need for a secret or "low profile" and "intense internally but relaxed externally" appearance [nei jin wai song]. [p153], which Colonel Jia explains is needed in order not to "excessively provoke other nations" and to maintain "China's positive international image."

Attacks to Deter

- NDU Book 3 on Space Warfare Campaigns – Attacks to Deter [2005]

1 – SHOCK AND AWE SPACE ATTACKS – [2005]
Yuan Zelu, *Space Warfare of the Joint Campaign*, Beijing: National Defense University Press, 2005.[24]

Constructing Space-Based Fire Networks
"Space-based fire networks are made up of the network systems of the various strike platforms that are in orbit. International space law prohibits this kind of weaponry deployment and even though space-based directed energy weapons and space-based kinetic energy weapons and other space-based weapons are successfully going through research and development, they still cannot be rapidly deployed in orbit. Nor are space flight units ready to go into outer space before they are ready, in order to avoid exposing operational plans and consume operational strength. For these reasons, emergency astronautic launches to organize the network will become the necessitated option for constructing a space-based fire network in wartime. In order to rapidly construct a space-based fire network in a future joint campaign, one must accomplish the following four things.

---

[23] Jia Junming, On Space Operations, NDU Press, Bejing. 2003. This book is on file at the USCC.
[24] Yuan Zelu was born in Oct 1966 in Xinjin, Sichuan Province. Entered the military in Sep 1985, graduated from the Air Force Missile Institute, Jul 1989, with a Bachelors Degree in Engineering; graduated from the Air Force Command Academy, Mar 1997, with a Master's Degree in Military Science; graduated from NDU, Jul 2003, with a Ph.D. in Military Science. Positions held, Platoon Commander, Deputy Company Commander, Staff Officer, etc, and currently NDU Deputy Regimental Staff Officer in the Training Department. He has published 18 academic works in *Military Science Journal*, *NDU Pictorial*, *Air Force Military Science Journal*, etc

First, one must research, develop, and test equipment for new types of astronautic carrier vehicles. The carrier rockets used today guarantee that the work will be extremely complex, that the launch preparation times will be several months in length, and that the needs of emergency astronautic launches will not be met. Consequently, research, development, and thorough equipment testing must ensure that carrier rockets, space shuttles, and other new types of aerospace craft are simpler and require less launch preparation time in order to greatly reduce launch preparation times and increase the rapid reaction capabilities of astronautic launch units and flight units.

Second, emergency/crisis launch and flight units must be set up. Space armies should set up emergency launch units and emergency flight units at a time that corresponds to the respective nation's new space carrier research and production situation. These units will shoulder the emergency astronautic launch tasks in wartime and ensure that a nation is able to rapidly construct space-based fire networks that fit with the operational requirements of the joint campaign in space.

Third, complete war preparation systems should be established. Emergency astronautic launch units and flight units should establish a complete set of war preparation duty institutions and weaponry and equipment and operational material preparation systems in order to maintain a regulated percentage of personnel in place and a percentage of good equipment. Moreover, corresponding with orders and instructions from higher levels, this war preparation system should be placed at the ready in order to guarantee that *on the day that it receives launch orders it will immediately be able to launch space-based fire platforms into orbit* and complete its networking tasks in the shortest amount of time. [Emphasis added]

Fourth, scientific and precise emergency launch plans and schemes must be formulated. Space army command offices, in accordance with the number of space-based fire platforms and the delivery capabilities of the astronautic launch and flight units, should thoroughly consider the effects of an opponent's space blockade and the weather conditions in the launch zone in order to formulate plans and schemes for multiple types of emergency astronautic launches. Moreover, adjustments must be made in a timely manner in accordance with the international political, diplomatic, and military struggle situations at the time of the war, so that the emergency astronautic launch activities proceed in a systematic manner, deliberately and not disorderly. This will guarantee that in the event of an opponent's space blockade or strike, one is able to rapidly deliver space-based weapon platforms into a designated orbit and make up a fire network.

ASAT from Ships and Submarines

Professor Liu Huanyu of Dalian Naval Academy: "Sea-Based Anti-Satellite Platform"25

"The development of military space system has enlarged the gap in sea power and posed a direct threat to sea power in the 21st century. In order for a country to intervene on the ocean, its sea power must be able to effectively suppress the function of the military space system. This paper proposes a sea-based platform

---

[25] Jianchuan Kexue Jishu, Feb 2004. Liu Huanyu of Dalian Naval Academy was born in Dalian, Liaoning in 1959. He has a master's degree in engineering, is an associate professor and a recipient of a number of military science and technology advancement awards. He has authored more than 10 research articles.

to counter enemy satellites. To develop this new type of operation platform for striking the war fighting power of the enemy, this will be a historical opportunity for raising a nation's sea power.

1. Anti-space warfare has become an important operation mission of a 21st century sea power

What China needs now is an effective capability to intervene on the ocean, which means a new sea power. The sea-based anti-satellite platform is a major component of the new sea power and must be given a high priority. If this new avenue is explored as soon as possible, China can hopefully improve its sea power dramatically within 10 years.

4. The sea-based anti-satellite platform proposal

4.1 Overall requirements of sea-based anti-satellite platform

The anti-satellite operation can be divided into the two levels of armed conflict and war. In a state of war there will be no constraints on the anti-missile system. In armed conflicts, the anti-satellite operation can be divided into low intensity and high intensity. Based on the maturity of anti-satellite missiles and their impact, there can be the following approaches:

(1) Low intensity armed conflicts

Jamming and blinding interference of surveillance satellites (including imaging satellites, electronic surveillance satellites, and ocean reconnaissance satellites), communication satellites, and navigation satellites.

(2) High intensity armed conflicts

Destructive attack of surveillance satellites in medium earth orbits and low earth orbits by directed energy weapons; command jamming and blinding of surveillance satellites, communication satellites, and early warning satellites in high orbits, and jamming of navigation and weather satellites.

Anti-satellite platforms can be divided into space-based platform and conventional platform (including land, sea, submarine, and air). The attack capability of space-based platforms is better but the cost is high, the payload is small, the platform is more vulnerable to jamming, and the adaptability is poor. Also, the deployment of space-based weapons platform is currently restricted by the rules for space arms race. The high level of operation makes space-based platforms only suitable for war. To disable the space military system of the enemy in an armed conflict, only the conventional platform can be used.

4.2 Anti-satellite nuclear submarine

….Nuclear submarines are not only well concealed but can sail for a long period of time. By deploying just a few anti-satellite nuclear submarines in the ocean, one can seriously threaten the entire military space system of the enemy. In addition to anti-satellite operations, these nuclear submarines can also be used for launching low orbit tactical micro-satellites to serve as powerful real time battlefield intelligence support. The main weakness of a submarine is that it is difficult to install detection systems on a submarine. Submarines have a weak capability for autonomous searching and therefore need the support of the national space monitoring system.

4.3 Anti-satellite cruisers

Surface ships built for anti-satellite operations can adopt more effective stealth technology and serve as a useful anti-satellite platform.

The main advantage of large anti-satellite ships is their strong autonomous searching capability. The platform can be equipped with not only spatial detection radar but also large scale electro-optical detection systems. The operations of anti-satellite ships are more complete and can effectively carry out electronic jamming. Anti-satellite cruisers are therefore an indispensable support force for a sea power.

Abstract: The development of military space system has enlarged the gap in sea power and posed a direct threat to sea power in the 21st century. In order for a country to intervene on the ocean, its sea power must be able to effectively suppress the function of the military space system. This paper proposes a sea-based platform to counter enemy satellites. To develop this new type of operation platform for striking the war fighting power of the enemy, this will be a historical opportunity for raising a nation's sea power.

3. Anti-satellite weapons

3.1 Electronic interference jamming

Electronic jamming of a satellite can be divided into hardware interference and command interference. Hardware jamming refers to electronic interference of passive and active surveillance equipment on electronic surveillance satellites that can lead to the disruption of the electronic surveillance function.

Command jamming refers to the jamming of the remote control and remote sensing systems of the military satellites. The operation of a spacecraft cannot take place without various commands and signals, but the communication system of all military satellites are easily jammed by the uplink and downlink. Jamming can at least greatly impair the satellite's performance. If the remote control command signal of the enemy satellite can be intercepted and decoded, then the remote control signal can be jammed so as to prevent the satellite from receiving ground command or to even alter the motion status of the satellite to make it deviate from the correct orbit, or to make it tumble and suffer permanent damage. Command interference is a cost-effective soft-kill weapon but the command signal of the enemy satellite must be intercepted and deciphered.

3.2 Anti-satellite directed energy weapons

Anti-satellite directed energy weapons include laser weapons, radio frequency weapons, and particle beam weapons.

3.2.1 Laser weapons

Anti-satellite laser weapons mainly employ two types of lasers: high energy laser and low energy laser. High energy lasers have a wavelength in the 1.06 to 10.6 μm range but mainly at 2.7 and 3.8 μm, and a continuous power of 1 to 10MW. A high energy laser can effectively destroy the electro-optical detectors, the optical system, the control surfaces, solar panels, and other structures of a satellite. When the laser intensity reaches or exceeds 300W/cm2, the surface of the optical glass of the satellite's electro-optical detector will begin to melt and the optics will fail. Generally a ground-based anti-satellite satellite laser weapon has a range of 500 - 1000km. The average power of the laser weapon should be more than 1000kW.

Low energy lasers are used for interfering with and temporarily blinding the electro-optical detectors of a satellite. For example, the CCD image transducer has a saturation threshold of only (100+/-10)mW/cm2 for lasers at a wavelength of 1.06☐m. Low energy lasers can also interfere and blind the infrared detector on early warning satellites and the electro-optical transducers on electro-optical reconnaissance satellites. Tests in the United States showed that even lasers of only tens of watts or hundreds of watts can effectively interfere with military reconnaissance satellites.

The United States, Russia, and others have made considerable achievements in the development of laser anti-satellite weapons and are technically capable of attacking satellites in low earth orbits. The "mid infrared chemical advanced laser" (MIRACL) developed by the United States Army is the world's first MW laser with a wavelength of 3.6 - 4.2☐m and a sustainable time as long as 3000 seconds. The system uses a SeaLite Beam Director (SLBD) and has a total weight of 12,712kg. In October 1997 the laser was successfully tested in an anti-satellite experiment conducted in the White sands missile range in New Mexico. The ground-based Russian lasers at Sary Shagan have also temporarily blinded some US satellites. These results have validated the effectiveness of anti-satellite laser weapons.

3.2.2 Radio frequency weapons

Radio frequency weapons refer mainly to high power microwave (HPM) weapons capable of generating extremely narrow, highly directional beam of radio frequency waves in the 100MHz to 100GHz range. When ground-based or space-based high power microwave weapons are used to attack enemy satellites, the microwave energy may be coupled through the front port (antenna) to the interior of the target satellite. Microwaves of longer wavelength may also couple through the rear port (openings and crevices in the satellite structure) to its interior. The microwave will be absorbed by the electronics in the satellite and cause great damage and disruption. In the meantime, the high temperature, strong ionization, radiation, and sound waves generated by the high power microwave can all lead to general damage of the satellite.

3.3 Hard impact weapons

3.3.1 Anti-satellite missiles

Anti-satellite weapons, based on their orbit, can be divided into two types: direct ascending and orbit sharing. The orbit sharing weapon is first deployed on the orbit of the target, then approaches the target at a low speed and destroys the target. Anti-satellite missiles were developed on the basis of anti-satellite missiles and could be launched on the ground, in the ocean, and from the air. The early anti-satellite weapons of the United States were mainly nuclear weapons. The U. S. military deployed the Thor ground-based anti-satellite missiles on Johnston Island in the Pacific from 1964 to 1975, but stopped the deployment because of high cost, limited effectiveness, large collateral damage, and constraints in usage. In the 1970s the United States began developing air-launched miniature vehicles (ALMV). The ALMV, also known as anti-satellite missile, was a two-stage missile with an automatic homing warhead. The kill mechanism was by high speed kinetic energy of the direct impact by the missile. Its operation altitude was below 1000km and the missile was released in the air from an F-15 fighter. The ALMV gained operating capability in the early 1990s but the project was terminated in March 1988 due to changes in the international situation and other technical and cost factors. The United States began developing kinetic energy anti-satellite (KE-ASAT) intercept missiles in the 1990s, aimed at ocean reconnaissance satellites of the former Soviet Union, with an interception altitude of 800 - 1000km. In August 1997, a prototype intercept missile locked onto the target in a simulation test.

3.3.2 Electromagnetic guns

Electromagnetic guns (EMG), also known as pulsed energy electromagnetic gun, can be divided into three different types: the coil gun, the orbit gun, and the reconnect gun. The coil gun was the early model of EMG; the current emphasis is on the orbit gun. The newest direction in EMG is the reconnect gun, a contact less electromagnetic launcher capable of accelerating a projectile in multiple stages. The development of EMG has been included by the United States defense department as a high priority technology project. The 90mm electromagnetic orbit gun of the United States Air Force has launched a 6kg projectile with an initial velocity of 2km/s in a test. The EMG is expected to launch 30 to 60mm projectiles weighing 5kg at a muzzle velocity of 4 to 8 km/second (giving 30 - 60 MJ of muzzle kinetic energy). However, the EMG technology today has not reached a practical level and has problems for being too bulky, too heavy, and too inefficient. With the development of superconductivity, there may be some breakthroughs in EMG technology. When the velocity of a projectile from a ground-launcher reaches 6 - 10km/s, it will be capable of directly shooting down satellites in 300 - 1000km low earth orbits.

4. The sea-based anti-satellite platform proposal

4.1 Overall requirements of sea-based anti-satellite platform

The effectiveness of a sea-based anti-satellite platform depends on the following three factors:

(1) The ability to destroy enemy space systems in a large area. The platform should have the ability to carry out sustained interference and attack so as to totally disable the space systems of the enemy in the war zone.

(2) The ability to survive. Like early warning planes, sea-based anti-satellite platforms are the "must kill" targets of the enemy. Survivability is therefore the first factor to consider in choosing a platform.

(3) The ability to move and fight a long term battle. High speed mobility is an important factor for a sea-based force to survive and maintain effective. The ability for long term operation is essential in fighting a war on the ocean.

4.2 Anti-satellite nuclear submarine

Currently there are two types of nuclear submarines: the strategic nuclear submarines as nuclear attack platforms, and the attack nuclear submarines used to eliminate strategic nuclear submarines. Both types serve nuclear wars and are strategic deterrents of a country. They are not used in conventional wars.

The construction costs of nuclear submarines are extremely high and few developing countries can afford them. Such an expensive platform must be used only at key places. In tactical uses, it does not pay to have a nuclear submarine carrying out anti-ship operations with a short range weapons like a torpedo.

Nuclear submarines are not only well concealed but can sail for a long period of time. By deploying just a few anti-satellite nuclear submarines in the ocean, one can seriously threaten the entire military space system of the enemy. In addition to anti-satellite operations, these nuclear submarines can also be used for launching low orbit tactical micro-satellites to serve as powerful real time battlefield intelligence support. The main weakness of a submarine is that it is difficult to install detection systems on a submarine. Submarines have a weak capability for autonomous searching and therefore need the support of the national space monitoring system.

4.3 Anti-satellite cruisers

Surface ships built for anti-satellite operations can adopt more effective stealth technology and serve as a useful anti-satellite platform.

The main advantage of large anti-satellite ships is their strong autonomous searching capability. The platform can be equipped with not only spatial detection radar but also large scale electro-optical detection systems. The operations of anti-satellite ships are more complete and can effectively carry out electronic jamming. Anti-satellite cruisers are therefore an indispensable support force for a sea power.

5. Conclusion

The effectiveness of a military power impacts a country's survival, development, and interest. The successful development of support weapons by China, such as the atomic and nuclear bombs and the satellite, has fundamentally changes China's military power and maintained the country's security. In today's international situation where military powers are badly lopsided and hegemony threatens world peace, China is in urgent need of new effective defense forces. Constrained by its national resources, the broad goals of economic development, and the international environment in the area, *it is impossible and unnecessary for China to develop large scale carriers. What China needs now is an effective capability to intervene on the ocean, which means a new sea power. The sea-based anti-satellite platform is a major component of the new sea power and must be given a high priority.* If this new avenue is explored as soon as possible, China can hopefully improve its sea power dramatically within 10 years.[Emphasis added.]

Attacking GPS Satellites and GPS Ground Stations

These recommendations are most surprising because the three authors show no concern about the vast economic catastrophe that destroying the GPS system would bring to the world. Rather, GPS appears to be merely a US military system. Chen Xuejun, Lang Daqiang: "Methods for Defeating GPS"][26] first ask:

"So what is the Achilles heel of GPS? An analysis of the working principles of GPS reveals three major weaknesses.

Defeating GPS at its Source: Exploiting the Weakness of the Low Orbit of Navigation Satellites

The navigation satellites of the GPS system consist of 24 low orbit small satellites, distributed on 6 nearly circular orbits with an inclination angle of 55 degrees. Each orbit has 4 satellites with an average altitude of only 16,000 kilometers, roughly equivalent to one half of that of a geosynchronous satellite. This low altitude provides an opportunity to locate, jam or destroy these navigation satellites. Off the shelf telescopes, sensors, and software, including computer controlled telescopes, can all observe these satellites. Amateur astronomers can follow and photograph GPS satellites. There are many ways to attack these satellites, with the following three most representative ones:

(1) Attack with anti-satellite satellites

---

[26] Yuan Guoxiong, Bai Tao, and Ren Zhang (Center of Precision Guidance Technology, Beijing University of Aeronautics and Astronautics, Beijing 100083): "A Hybrid Reentry Guidance Method for Space-Based Ground Attack Weapon System"; Authors: Yuan Guoxiong (1968 -), armament department engineer of PLA Unit 96211, lieutenant colonel, currently a master's student at the Institute of Automation Science and Electrical Engineering of Beijing University of Aeronautics; research interest in precision missile guidance technology and space-based trajectory weapon guidance technology Ren Zhan is a professor, doctoral advisor, and Chang Jiang Scholar. Military Digest, Junshi Wenzhai in Chinese 1 Nov 04, pp 52-53

There are two ways to attack with an anti-satellite satellite. One is by suicide attack. In a suicide attack, an anti-satellite satellite carries conventional explosive and approaches the navigation satellite. When it is near the GPS satellite, it is exploded either by remote control from the ground or by itself and takes the GPS satellite with it. The other method is to use the satellite as a weapon platform and install missile launchers or rapid firing guns on it. When the GPS satellite is within the range of the weapons on board, shots are fired to destroy the GPS satellite. The United States military estimates that more than one half of the anti-satellite tests conducted by the former Soviet Union had succeeded.

(2) Attack with high energy laser weapons

High energy laser weapons can be space based or ground based. Space based high energy laser weapons have the best attack results. Laser weapons attack the GPS satellites by burning and destroying the target. Space based platforms can usually be deployed at an altitude of 1000 kilometer or more in order to reduce atmospheric attenuation of the laser beam and to ensure that the lasers have sufficient energy. Using laser weapons, the navigation satellites can be destroyed by burning from the front, the side, or the back.

(3) Attack with high altitude weather monitoring rocket
An ordinary inexpensive weather monitoring rocket may carry a bomb containing a large amount of small lead shots into a designated orbit. Once exploded, the small lead shots will fly out with a relative velocity of 6.4 kilometers per second and destroy any satellite they encounter. When a few kilograms of gravel are thrown into orbit, they will attack the satellites like meteor showers and incapacitate the expensive GPS constellation.

Defeating GPS in the Middle: Exploiting the Scattered and Exposed Ground Stations

A GPS system cannot position or navigate without a ground control system. Once the ground control is damaged, it would no longer be able to accurately guide or navigate long range weapons. The ground control of a GPS system consists of a main control station (located in Colorado in the United States), three feeder stations (Kwajalein in the Pacific Ocean, Diego Garcia in the Indian Ocean, and Ascension Island in the Atlantic Ocean) and five monitoring stations (Hawaiian Islands plus the four locations mentioned above). The monitoring stations are unmanned and are responsible for acquiring the satellite observation data and transfer them to the main control… Since they are widely scattered, the normal operation will be disrupted if any one part of the entire system is attacked. Therefore, submarine launched missiles or long range weapons can be used to attack these stations, or the special forces may be trained to effectively infiltrate and destroy the stations.

Defeating GPS at the End: Exploiting the Fact that Navigation Signals Are Highly Attenuated

GPS subscribers achieve their positioning and navigation by relying on the wireless radio waves and navigation messages from the satellite to the orbit. Radio waves can easily be jammed; atmospheric and solar spot activities can interfere with the normal transmission. The transmitting power is usually only a few tens of watts…By covering up the encoding information transmitted by the satellite, the precision weapons guided by the GPS will lose its accuracy and miss the target. It is simple and inexpensive to build a jammer." [27]

Orbital Missiles to Attack Earth Targets

Author Zhao Ruian has not been identified, but his article merits lengthy quoting because of his mastery

---

[27] An earlier study was found by Dean Cheng. Zhu Rinzhong, "The Theory of GPS and Methods of Countering It," *Junshi xueshu*, May 1999, pp. 5859, in Dean Cheng, "The Chinese Space Program: A 21st Century Fleet in Being," in James Mulvenon and Andrew Yang, *A Poverty of Riches: New Challenges and Opportunities in PLA Research*, Santa Monica: RAND, 2003, p. 46.

of the details of space weapons and his recommendations in "The Concept of Orbital Ballistic Missile"[28]

Orbital ballistic missile (orbital missile) is a new-concept strategic ballistic missile is a multi-task, multi-role attack weapon capable of implementing random orbit transfer from earth orbits and can serve the function of an intercontinental ballistic missile, an anti-satellite weapon, and an orbital bomber weapon.

This new-concept strategic missile is no longer a ballistic missile in the original sense, but is a cross between a ballistic missile and a satellite; it is a ballistic missile in a satellite orbit or a satellite with weapons capability….The concept of orbital ballistic missile bears resemblance to the idea of the Common Aero Vehicle (CAV) proposed by the Air Armament Center of the Eglin Air Force Base in the United States. The idea is for an orbital system under attack to launch a number of CAVs into slow Earth orbits and, when necessary, make them deviate from their orbits. Through guidance, navigation, and aerodynamic control in the atmosphere, the CAVs can release their warheads from certain geometric locations

For China's national security, it is undoubtedly important to study the development status pf space weapons in the world and to investigate the ideas and related technologies of orbital ballistic missiles."

An orbital missile is a new-concept strategic ballistic missile is a multi-task, multi-role attack weapon capable of implementing random orbit transfer from earth orbits and can serve the function of an intercontinental ballistic missile, an anti-satellite weapon, and an orbital bomber weapon.

This new-concept strategic missile is no longer a ballistic missile in the original sense, but is a cross between a ballistic missile and a satellite; it is a ballistic missile in a satellite orbit or a satellite with weapons capability. It integrates the function of a missile and a satellite and is capable of transferring into or from an earth orbit. With that, the rigorous boundary between a satellite and a missile has disappeared. In the development of strategic missiles, our thinking should be directed toward space and we should recognize that, as far as orbits are concerned, a satellite can become a missile and vice versa. Whether the warhead is nuclear or non-nuclear, kinetic or directed energy, the boundary should be knocked down and mature technologies of satellite and missiles should be integrated with new technologies of the future. Orbital ballistic missiles should be developed using the mutually interchangeable ground-based and space-based missiles, ground-ground missiles, and anti-satellite missiles. They would greatly enhance the deterrent power of strategic ballistic weapons. From an engineering technology perspective, the idea of converting missiles into satellites and converting satellites into missiles is rather obvious. However, a deeper examination of the concept can shed light on the internal conflicts and evolution of space weapons and initiate new paradigms.

The concept of orbital ballistic missile bears resemblance to the idea of the Common Aero Vehicle (CAV) proposed by the Air Armament Center of the Eglin Air Force Base in the United States. The idea is for an orbital system under attack to launch a number of CAVs into slow Earth orbits and, when necessary, make them deviate from their orbits. Through guidance, navigation, and aerodynamic control in the atmosphere, the CAVs can release their warheads from certain geometric locations. The idea of CAV came from the study of powered re-entry vehicles. CAVs can definitely be launched from sub-orbital carrier rockets, such as ICBMs. The orbital ballistic missile is an extension of the center stage of a powered ballistic missile. It can actually be not in the orbit and its flight can straddle the atmosphere. For

---

[28] Zhongguo Hangtian in Chinese 01 Jan 04 ,Zhao Ruian: "The Concept of Orbital Ballistic Missiles."

this reason orbital ballistic missiles also bear some resemblance to the HyperSoar [previous name published in English] proposed recently by the Lawrence Livermore National Laboratory of the United States. HyperSoar is a re-usable, sub-orbital aerovehicle that can release weapons at orbital speed using rocket engines.

The basic issues of the orbital ballistic missile system can be summarized as follows:

1. In the post booster stage and the free flight stage, the orbital ballistic missile must be able to detect, recognize, and classify incoming enemy missiles and to receive signals from early warning systems and to intercept missiles.

2. The orbital ballistic missiles must be able to track and verify the orbit of an intercepting missile, to determine whether the intercepting missile is on the collision coursed of the orbital missile, and to forecast the collision time.

3. If an interception is about to occur, the orbital missile must initiate evasive action based on ground commands or autonomous detection in a timely and accurate manner. Once an evasive action is taken, the orbital missile must achieve a miss distance greater than the kill radius of the interceptor, or enter a holding orbit that revolves around the Earth, or climb above the Earth's atmosphere.

4. If the decision is to take evasive action, then there must also be a plan to return to the original orbit so that its munitions can accomplish its attack action according to the planned accuracy. If the orbital missile is to enter an orbit that revolves around the Earth, or crosses the Earth's atmosphere, then the new position for attacking the target must be accurately determined and the final orbit correction and attack mission (ground or air) must be re-planned.

5. If the intercepting missile of the enemy is expected to change course, or if additional interception missile are expected, there must be plans to preserve and protect the fuel and electric power of the orbital ballistic missile.

6. If the plan for launch is cancelled, then the munitions of the orbital ballistic missile will be pushed into deep space.

A new paradigm of orbital ballistic missile, a concept different from orbital weapons, has emerged. It can greatly enhance the agility, stealth, and penetrating power of the sub-orbital ICBMs. It re-enters the atmosphere to attack ground targets with a small at an exceedingly high speed; making it essentially impossible to intercept. It can put the missile defense system in a bind and provide a new platform for various new non-nuclear munitions. Here we are in no hurry to consider whether current or future engineering technologies are capable of making orbital ballistic missiles a reality. A foreign military expert has put it well: "Let us not focus our attention on feasibility; strategic foresights will make new technologies emerge miraculously."

Space Superiority Mission of Orbital Ballistic Missiles

One of the main missions in space control ("space superiority") is anti-satellite. The development of anti-satellite systems has had a history of many years. They are now capable of destroying enemy surveillance satellites, electronic reconnaissance satellites, weather satellites, and navigation satellites. The investment in this area has been sporadic due to the restriction of international treaties and the technical challenges of an anti-satellite system for greater altitude, farther distance, and the handling of "MIRVed" warheads.

However, all countries in the world have shown a sustained interest in anti-satellite defense because of its implication in space superiority…..

To attack a target satellite, the orbital ballistic missile may climb to the intercept point or it may enter a holding orbit revolving around the Earth, and then to encounter the target by changing the orbit. The advantages of the direct-climb approach are that it is simple, its early warning time is short, and its fuel-to-mass ratio is low. However, the approach has the disadvantage that each launch can only have one chance of attack. In contrast, the approach of attacking from the orbit can have several chances of encounter in a single day.

The possible operations are: (1) making the orbit of the orbital ballistic missile coaxial with the orbit of the target satellite, and achieving an interception by expanding the orbit with thrust impulse; (2) placing the orbital ballistic missile in an Earth orbit lower than that of the target satellite, so that its apogee is almost coincident with the perigee of the target satellite's orbit, and intercepting the target by means of the faster orbital speed of the missile; and (3) still placing the orbital ballistic missile into an Earth orbit lower than that of the target, but intercepting the target satellite at a certain orbit position by means of a dynamic jump. The advantage of the orbital interception plan is that it provides multiple changes for interception, and that the orbit of the target satellite can be determined and tracked accurately before the attack. However, it requires a more complex control technology and that it needs a higher fuel-to-mass ratio. The target satellite will also have a longer early warning period.

As early as 40 years ago, there have been research and testing of ICBM equipped with nuclear warhead for attacking satellites on their climb up. It was reported that the explosion of the nuclear warhead created an artificial radiation layer that indiscriminately destroyed satellites over a fairly long period of time. This "kill all" approach did not receive much support; instead, conventional warheads (explosive warhead, fragmental warhead, and continuous rod warhead) seemed to offer a better compromise between the complexity of the detonator and the effectiveness of the explosion. A fragmental warhead consists of the explosive and a shell; the fracture of the shell releases a large amount of fragments when the explosive is detonated. It is estimated that 500g of any material traveling at a speed of 3 km/s has an equivalent kinetic energy equal to 500g of high explosive. Satellites are fragile structures moving at high speed; they can be easily damaged by a small mass moving at a relatively modest velocity.

Another approach is to create a mesh of small fragments across the satellite orbit with a small amount of explosives. The fragments are held by metal wires or fiber threads. The effect of gravity may be countered with a small thrust and the mesh can be extended to a diameter of 30 m and maintained for about 1.7 seconds. For a 15kg warhead containing a detonator, 5 kg of fragments, and other mesh material, the 5 kg of fragments can be 5,700 steel cubes of 5mm size distributed at a density of one per 12 mm. This type of expanded mesh warhead can tolerate a greater detonation error and afford a greater probability of kill.

Although laser weapons can travel thousands of kilometers of distance at the speed of light and destroy targets instantaneously, without the constraint of orbital dynamics and aimed at any target within the line of sight, but it is still not practical to use laser as on-board weapons for satellites. Aside from the technological obstacles, the weight of tons of materials required by hydrogen fluoride and oxygen iodide chemical lasers, under development in some foreign countries, can cost $2 billion and weigh 17.5 tons. Therefore, the on-board anti-satellite mission calls for a new paradigm in high-energy laser weapons.

The Deterrent Mission of Orbital Ballistic Missiles

No matter what are the initial velocity and the angle of inclination for orbital ballistic missiles, their paths are always sub-orbits consisting of sections of conical curves and covering less than one revolution around the Earth. The initial velocities are less than the orbital velocity of 7.9 km/s. If the initial velocity reaches the orbital velocity, the flight locus will become a circular orbit. Any further increase in the initial velocity will change the circular orbit into an elliptical orbit. For an initial velocity of 9 km/s, the apogee will exceed 5,000 km. With an initial velocity of 7.2 km/s, an orbital ballistic missile will climb to an altitude of 1320 km.

When an orbital ballistic missile follows the command and enters a holding orbit, the deterrent mission of bombing from the orbit will involve slowing down it speed and launching the secondary munitions. While converting the kinetic energy corresponding to the high velocity (5 to 10 km/s) of the weapon, the resulting power and heat destroys the ground target. In order to reach a velocity of 10 km/s, the altitude of the holding orbit must exceed 40,000 km. Weapons at that altitude will take 5 hours to reach the ground. A low-orbit weapon will afford the enemy only a short reaction time. A weapon launched from orbit 1,000 km high is estimated to reach the ground in about 45 minutes. A compromise is to place the weapons on low-Earth orbits at 300 to 400 km high and to obtain a 5 km/s collision velocity.

The projectiles launched from the holding orbit may be in the form of thin long rods, super-hard penetrators, and local-kill charges. Thin rod projectiles may be used against hard targets that are not deeply buried. The penetration mechanism is a combination of cumulative burning by the sharp tip of the projectiles and cumulative burning of the material being penetrated. The pressure generated at the tip of the projectile will melt the target locally. The projectiles are generally thin rods of heavy metals 1 to 2 meters long with a penetration depth of 2 to 3 times its length. A 20 kg 2-meter rod can penetrate the target 6 to 8 meters. This is equivalent to detonating 20 kg of high explosives in a well whose diameter is slightly larger than the rod diameter. As soon as the rod enters the target, it becomes a heap of debris. The super-hard penetration projectile is a short ablation rod with an explosive tip. When it reaches a preset depth or enters a low resistance zone (house or tunnel), it detonates a timed fuse.

The materials suitable for making ablation rods, such as carbon and tungsten, cannot generally tolerate a speed much faster than 1.5 km/s. Some new materials under development, such as nanometer laminated material, may raise the impact velocity to greater than 4.3 km/s. This capability has now been verified. This type of orbital missiles can be used against hard targets buried underground to a depth of hundreds of meters and with structures hardened against nuclear attack.

For orbital missiles, it is difficult to attack small, hardened targets even when their positions can be accurately determined. The projectile must have an aim high accurate and un-deviated by atmospheric fluctuation. To be accurate, the projectile must be launched from a precise position and with an accurate velocity. Today's ICBMs have greatly improved accuracy, but 100-meter accuracy, although more than adequate for a nuclear warhead, is not accurate enough for penetrating a hardened target. Since the re-entry at a speed of 4.6 km/s will produce plasmas around the vehicle and blocks type I communication signals, the final stage guidance must be modified to use inertia measurement plus GPS or to use star light positioning and ground infrared systems.

Practical Issues of Orbital Ballistic Missiles

The first problem faced by orbital ballistic missiles is that they are much heavier than a nuclear warhead. Approximately 90 percent of the weight comes from the fuel for the thruster. It remains to be seen how the mass of other components can be proportionally reduced so that the warhead structure can withstand the flight load. The electric servo for control must be able to handle the guidance and control inputs. These issues must rely on technological innovations and advancement, including on-board autonomous monitoring systems, autonomous control system, super-precision inertia guidance system, high power orbital thruster, and new R& D results in nuclear warheads.

Here we would make a special mention of the classical research done by Qian Xuesen 50 years ago on constant continuous low thrust orbit in a central force field. This was a concept advanced by Qian 6 years before the former Soviet Union launched the first artificial satellite. Qian's work has received wide attention and was extensively studied for decades. In particular, Qian proved the existence of the critical acceleration in a constant continuous radial thrust. Above this critical value, the satellite met the escape condition and its orbit is a tightly spiraling intergalactic orbit. Below this critical acceleration, the vehicle in a circular orbit will spiral along the tangent and reach a maximum altitude. If the radial thrust continues and exceeds this point, the vehicle will spiral back and returns to the initial altitude. Although the return orbit is totally different from the outward orbit, their transfer times are equal. This is the so-called "somersault" orbit of the spacecraft. If the radial thrust suddenly stops at the moment of maximum altitude, the subsequent orbit will be an ellipse. This orbit needs a miniature electric rocket engine; exploratory studies have yet to be initiated to determine how such an orbit may be exploited for aborting a launch and for orbital movement in the mid-stage of an orbital ballistic missile.

Conclusion

Nikita Khrushchev, prime minister of the former Soviet Union, had said something 40 years ago that continues to impress US military experts today: "When the imperialists ponder whether to launch a nuclear war, the Sword of Damocles hangs over their heads." Forty years later, all the countries in the world discovered that the Sword of Damocles can be hanging over their heads any time. Although the "Cold War" no longer exists, but the potential danger still weighs heavily in people's mind.

Commander Lance Lord of the United States Space Command recently wrote in Aviation Week and Space Technology that, "If we wish to be victorious in the war, this asymmetric superiority in space must be with the Army, the Navy, the Air Force, and the Marines. We must continue to devote material, effort, and personnel to these goals, and we have the talents to exploit this 'absolute high ground' of space."

For China's national security, it is undoubtedly important to study the development status pf space weapons in the world and to investigate the ideas and related technologies of orbital ballistic missiles."

Plasma Attack Against Low-Orbit Spy Satellites [29]

Professor Yang Juan stops just short of explicitly recommending plasma attacks for China, yet her enthusiasm for demonstrating the feasibility of this approach seems obvious.

"This paper studies the effectiveness of using plasma to interrupt low-orbit reconnaissance satellite operations and proposes a scheme for using plasma against satellites. Analysis of satellite charging and discharging effects and mechanisms in a plasma environment indicates that plasma damages low-orbit satellites by causing arc-discharging potential differences to form on the surface of a satellite and that produces strong arc currents and electromagnetic pulses that damage solar cells, surface temperature control materials, microwave and electronic instruments on a satellite, and disrupts normal antenna operations. This study divided a satellite surface into 14 different equivalent parts, and using equivalent charging modes, calculated the charging processes of high-density low-energy and medium-energy plasmas on the satellite surfaces, analyzed the effects of electron temperature and density, the initial potential of satellite surfaces, and solar cell array potential on the final equilibrium potential reached on the satellite surfaces.

A concept of using plasmas against low-orbit satellites has recently been proposed based on the interference and damage effects they have on satellites (Refs. 1, 2). The basic idea is to release a cloud of high-density plasma in front of a satellite, and when the satellite passes through it, the charged particles in the plasma will cause the charges carried on the surface of the satellite to form certain potential differences which will produce surface arc discharges that will disrupt the normal operating state of the satellite. The plasma will also create reactive power loss in the solar cells, which will debilitate the electronic equipment on the satellite. This paper will proceed from the aspect of the discharges on a satellite surface caused by plasma, and through computation analysis will study the feasibility of this idea.

---

[29] Journal of Northwestern Polytechnical University, pp 93-97, article by Yang Juan, Su Weiyi, Mao Genwang, and He Hongqing (College of Astronautics, Northwestern Polytechnical University, Xian 710072): "On Calculating Effectiveness of Plasma Defense Against Low-Orbit Spy Satellite"; Yang Juan (1963-), female, assistant professor, Doctorate holder, researches rocket launchers and plasma applications.

Satellites Designed with Stealth[30]

"There is a great deal of work to do to develop a stealth satellite. In this paper, the optical signatures of a satellite and its stealth related issues were preliminarily explored. A number of schemes were proposed. The rationality and feasibility of these schemes need to be jointly investigated with relevant experts.

"The optical characteristics of satellite were analyzed. The analysis showed that the sun is the primary influencing factor of satellite temperature. Satellites mainly emit infrared radiation [IR] in the mid to far IR region, and reflect sunlight in the visible region. Finally, methods to conceal such optical signatures of satellites were preliminarily explored.

Optically Stealth Satellite

In theory, optical stealth refers to blending the optical signatures of a target into the background so that detectors cannot pick up the target from its background. In contrast to outer space, the optical signatures of a satellite, either in the IR or visible region, are so much more prominent. It would be extremely difficult to conceal itself by controlling the emissivity and reflectivity at the surface of a satellite. This creates the following dilemma. In order to minimize visible light emitting from the satellite, it is necessary to curtail reflected sunlight. However, this move will raise the temperature of the satellite. Its IR radiation will go up in intensity. It is difficult to take care of visible light and infrared radiation at the same time. The following areas need to be

it is possible to select a proper satellite surface material in designing a stealth satellite. This material should have very a low emissivity at these atmospheric windows. In addition, it should have a very high emissivity in other non-window regions of the IR spectrum, which will also enhance heat dissipation by radiation in these non-window regions to lower the temperature of the satellite.

As for sunlight reflected by satellite, it is possible to keep satellite reflected sunlight away from the Earth, especially away from optical observation stations operated by potential opponents, by adopting a suitable design. If a satellite is spherical in shape, a portion of the sunlight will be reflected toward the Earth. To this end, a polyhedron design ought to be employed to the extent possible so that the attitude of the satellite may be adjusted in orbit to prevent reflected sunlight from propagating towards the Earth. Solar panels used to supply power to the satellite must also be designed with stealth in mind. Diffuse refection from the satellite surface should be avoided, and specular reflection should be employed instead.

Design the satellite in such a way so that it looks like a piece of space junk. There are numerous objects orbiting around the earth today. If a satellite is designed to look like a piece of space junk, it will minimize the interest of our enemy in such a satellite in order to render more protection to our satellite.

In contrast to the cold outer space environment, the optical signatures of a satellite are especially prominent. There is a great deal of work to do to develop a stealth satellite. In this paper, the optical signatures of a satellite and its stealth related issues were preliminarily explored. A number of schemes

---

[30] Hefei *Guang Dianzi Jishu yu Xinxi* in Chinese 01 Aug 04; Li Yubo, Lu Yuan and Ling Yongshun (Institute of Electronic Engineering, Hefei, Anhui 230037, China): "Research on Optical Characteristics of Satellites and Camouflage;" Li Yubo is a lecturer at the Institute of Electronic Engineering, engaged in research on computer and optoelectronic detection.

were proposed. The rationality and feasibility of these schemes need to be jointly investigated with relevant experts.

Space Electronic Jamming [31]

1 Introduction

In future space countermeasure environments, the emergence and fielding of large numbers of anti-satellite weapons will pose threat to the survivability of satellite systems. In addition, since the quantity of fuel carried by satellites is limited, it is impossible for satellites to conduct multiple large scope orbital maneuvers. As a result, they have limited ability to evade external attacks. In order to improve the survivability of satellites and spacecraft, it is necessary to develop satellites with space electronic reconnaissance and countermeasure capabilities. The main purpose of space-borne electronic reconnaissance systems are to conduct general surveys of the opponent's ground and sea surface electronic equipment, as well as defend itself or the spacecraft protected by it, thereby improving survivability and integrated operational capability of the friendly side. In order to occupy a place in space-based information warfare, space-borne electronic reconnaissance and countermeasure equipment should possess the following abilities: the ability to detect and locate space electromagnetic radiation sources, the ability to intercept complex space signals, and the ability to carry out electronic jamming.

2 Space-borne Electronic Reconnaissance and Electronic Countermeasure Systems

"In the complicated space environment, a space-borne electronic reconnaissance and electronic countermeasure system that can operate safely should contain at least several basic functional modules: the passive location module, the active radar detection module, the complex signal detection, sorting and processing module, and the electronic jamming module.

2.4 Space-borne Electronic Jamming Techniques

Deception type jamming is primarily used to confuse radar's automatic detection system. It generates ghost signals that simulate real signal parameters to make it difficult for the automatic tracking system of the radar to select the real target from the acquired signals. Its strong point is that the utilization ratio of the jamming power is relatively high. It can also deceive the radar imperceptibly. Retransmission type jamming based on DDS or DRFM can be used for deception type jamming. The basic principles of both of these two types of jamming are modulation, copying and retransmission of the received radar signals. It is not necessary, therefore, to gain more knowledge of the radar signal parameters and the operating mode of the radar. However, once detected, deception jamming loses effect. In addition, the jamming

-----

[31] Nanjing *Hangtian Dianzi Duikang* in Chinese 01 Aug 06 pp 22-24; Zhang Fenghui, Yao Chongbin (No. 804 Institute of Shanghai Academy of Spaceflight Technology, Shanghai 200082): "Spaceborne Electronic Reconnaissance and Countermeasures"; Zhang Fenghui (1977-), male, with master's degree, engaged in the work of signal processing, as well as electronic reconnaissance and countermeasures; Yao Chongbin (1967-), male, research fellow, engaged in the work of radar reception and radar electronic countermeasures. "Aerospace Electronic Warfare," bimonthly periodical sponsored by Institute 8511 of China Aerospace Science and Industry Corporation (CASIC) focusing on electronic/optoelectronic offense and defense and countermeasure technologies for electronic equipment and systems such as radar, guidance and detonators, communication, navigation, and C3I related to aircraft and missile weapon systems.

will not affect the detection of real targets by phased array radar in search mode; it can only increase false alarms.

It is necessary to be flexible in practical applications. Based on the actual situation, either one jamming measure or the combination of the two jamming measures can be implemented.

3 Conclusion

In a signal environment that is becoming more and more complicated every day, it is impossible for space-based electronic reconnaissance systems to rely on a certain single reconnaissance measure to carry out location and detection of the radiation source signals. It must adopt the mode that integrates a variety of techniques, such as passive, active and low interception probability techniques. The detection and sorting of electromagnetic signals must not rely on a single analytical method, either. It is necessary to utilize the advantages of all kinds of algorithms to acquire optimal detection results through integrated analytical processing. In addition, the reconnaissance system must also be able to counter jamming and release effective jamming. Otherwise, the space-based reconnaissance system does not possess survivability in a modern warfare environment.

Six Studies on Jamming US Classified Data Links [JTIDS] [2005]

The following six articles suggest a clear focus on disabling US command and control in wartime.

"Optimization of Spread Spectrum Code and Design of Spread Spectrum Pattern of JTIDS" –

1 This article from the 2005, 5th issue of Xiandai Fangyu Jishu [Modern Defence Technology] by Shi Wenhui, Zhang Hui, and Lai Weilin of the School of Telecommunication Engineering, Xian University of Electronic Science and introduces the general concept of jamming the US JTIDS, making clear the significance of such an operation..

"Reconnaissance and Jamming to US Military Tactical Digital Information Link (TADIL) A" –

2 This article from the 2005, 4th issue of Ship Electronic Engineering by Cai Xiao of Department of Electronics and Information Engineering, HUST, and Unit 63888 of PLA (Jiyuan, Henan), Guo Wei of Department of Electronics and Information Engineering, HUST (Wuhan, Hubei 430074), and Zhou Yingfang of Institute of Computer Science, HUST, introduces the work mechanism, the equipment, transmission and reception, and the information transmission frame format and work model of TADIL A. It proposes two methods of attacking TADIL A, as a picket station and as a control station. In the former case, "reception only is carried out first to reconnoiter all the activities in the network and to obtain the number of the picket stations in the network and the addresses they use; during the second query cycle, adjust the local address in a timely manner for interception of the tactical information sent by the control station and the picket stations; decode the encrypted information with reference to the unencrypted information; goniometrically locate a picket station of the enemy to be jammed or destroyed. Under the assumed identity of said picket station, sent a reply message to the control station. The opponent is deceived by the false information and the objective of the attack is thus achieved." In the second case, "reconnoiter the network activities and record the order of the addresses of the roll calls. If no information is available, set up a network using the identity of a control station. The number of the addresses increases from few to many in steps until the 63 addresses are used up. If no reply is received from any picket

station, try again using a different frequency until a picket station replies, then <u>assume the identity of the control station</u> to control the network operation. If a control station is present and working, it is goniometricaly located, jammed or destroyed by firepower, and then take over its control of the network." "Shipboard Electronic Countermeasures" is a bimonthly periodical sponsored by China Shipbuilding Industry Corporation (CSIC), 723rd Research Institute in Yangzhou, Jiangsu, and featuring academic studies and technical reports on electronic warfare, radar, signal processing, and related technologies.

3 "Study of Datalink and Its Countermeasures" –

This article from the 2004, 6th issue of Jianchuan Dianzi Duikang [Shipboard Electronic Countermeasure] by Zhai Lichao and Lu Jiuming of Electronic Engineering Institute of PLA (Hefei, Anhui 230037) introduces the datalink systems used by foreign armed forces, specifically Link 4A, Link 11, Link 14, and Link 16. It lists the characteristics of these systems and, based on these, several jamming methods. For jamming methods based on frequency-hopping communication, jamming by tracking and aiming, jamming by waveform aiming and jamming by broadband comb-like blocking are mentioned, with the last one described as "the only effective jamming method for high-speed frequency-hopping communication." <u>There are three ways of realizing electronic jamming of space-based datalink:</u> "first, to conduct electronic jamming of the datalink information system and equipment of the enemy space platforms from one's own space platforms; second, to conduct jamming of the used in the land, sea and space platforms of the enemy datalink terminals; third, to conduct electronic jamming of the military electronic information system and equipment used in the enemy space platforms from land, sea, and space." Means of conducting satellite-based network attacks include: paralyzing the enemy's information equipment for transmission, processing and command and control so that the overall datalink information capacity of the enemy cannot be coordinated for operation, thereby greatly reducing its overall combat ability; decoding the monitor and control command codes of the enemy information system, sending misleading commands to the enemy spacecraft to paralyze the enemy's communication equipment and information processing equipment." Finally, the article states that high-performance microwave weapons, laser weapons and solid nuclear, kinetic energy, directional energy weapons, anti-satellite satellites and new concept satellite countermeasure weapons can be used for attacks on the electronic equipment and personnel of the enemy.

4 "Study of Optimal Jamming of JTIDS" –

This article from the 2004, 8th issue of Wuxian Dian Gongcheng [Radio Engineering] by Wang Hui, Zeng Xingwen, and Shen Zhenning of the Electronic Engineering Institute of PLA (Hefei, Anhui 230037) proposes an optimal plan for jamming JTIDS. Following a complete analysis of the anti-jamming properties of JTIDS, specifically its key parameters such as tamed spread spectrum, frequency hop and timing jitter, etc., the authors conduct simulation tests using Matlab, comparing jamming results in different jamming modes. The "simulation results agree with the theoretical analysis, i.e., with the greatest savings in power as the starting point, the optimal jamming plan can be obtained with sawtooth wave modulation combined with waveform coincidence." The authors conclude that "theoretically, this method requires the least amount of power for jamming."

#5 "Study of JTIDS Signal Jamming Techniques" –

This article from the 2004, 4th issue of Hangtian Dianzi Duikang [Aerospace Electronic Warfare] by Cai Xiaoxia, Chen Hong, Guo Jianlian, and Wang Keren of the Electronic Engineering Institute of PLA (Hefei, Anhui 230037) states that two factors -- reconnaissance and interference -- must be considered for jamming JTIDS signals. According to their characteristics, reconnaissance of the JTIDS signals comprises mainly of monitoring and receiving the DS signals, which must be done with a broadband reconnaissance receiver.

6 "Study of JTIDS Jamming" –

This article from the 2004, 3rd issue of Hangtian Dianzi Duikang [Aerospace Electronic Warfare] by Zhang Xin and Yang Shaoquan of the Electronic Warfare Institute, Xian Electronic Science and Technology University (Xian, Shaanxi 710071) proposes several methods for jamming JTIDS based on JTIDS and its anti-jamming measures: block jamming, prediction jamming and correlation jamming.

Ten Studies of Kinetic Kill Vehicles [2005]

The following summaries of ten articles from various PRC academic journals on China's kinetic kill vehicle research set up a framework ---

 # 1 "Simulation Modeling Research For Kinetic Kill Vehicle" -- This article from the 2005, 8th issue of *Wei Jisuanji Xinxi* [*Control and Automation*] by author Zhang Aiyu of the Department of Automatic Control, School of Automation, Beijing University of Aviation and Aerospace, says that six-degree-of-freedom modeling and simulation techniques are essential to the guidance design of a kinetic kill vehicle [KKV]. The trajectory movement dynamics and attitude movement dynamics models are provided for the KKV, as well as a mathematical model of the complete guidance and control system. The paper says using the Simulink simulation tools provided by MATLAB, simple and effective model construction can be achieved where "the simulation process is interactive, the parameters can be randomly configured and the simulation results after corrections, which can be analyzed and are viewable, can be quickly obtained." The simulation results based on a certain type of KKV prove the validity of the simulation model.

 # 2 "A Study of Kinetic Interceptor Attitude Control System Based on Feedback Linearization" -- This article from the 2005, 3rd issue of *Yuhang Xuebao* [*Journal of Astronautics*] by authors Wang Qingchao and Li Da of Harbin Institute of Technology, says that when a kinetic interceptor enters into terminal guidance it has to maneuver with large angles. The interceptor attitude system at this phase is characterized by nonlinearity, strong-coupling and MIMO. The study says it is vital for the kinetic interceptor to adjust its attitude quickly and precisely in this phase by maintaining the target within the sight of its homing device while adjusting the center of mass of the interceptor to ensure its final collision with the target. Using the adaptive inverse controllers integrated with PID neural networks, the interceptor can quickly and precisely track a given signal while conducting large angle maneuvering and hit the target. "*Journal of Astronautics*," a bimonthly periodical managed by the Association for Science and Technology, sponsored by Chinese Society of Astronautics, and features research notes and commentaries on scientific and technological developments in spacecraft, satellites, missiles, rockets, and related subsystems.

 # 3 "Concept of Kinetic Orbit Weapons **and Its Development"** -- This study from the 2005, 2nd issue of *Xiandai Fangyu Jishu* [*Modern Defence Technology*] by authors Wan Ziming [Tel.: (010)68389378], Yang Yuguang, and Deng Longfan of the Second Research Academy of China Aerospace Science & Industry Corporation [CASIC], Second System Design Department, says that space forces will inevitably become a major new military branch judging from the history and future trend of development of Russian and US space forces. The basic concept of the kinetic orbit weapon and its position and effect as a "new means of strategic deterrence" are discussed in the study.

The current situation and future development of kinetic orbit weapons in Russia and the United States are described with the note that the "control of space will become the premises for the control of air, sea and land and weaponization of space will be an inevitable developmental trend." The developmental requirements and available targets are analyzed, specifically anti-satellite weapons developed as defense against military satellites and other space-based threats; space-based kinetic self-defense weapons developed to counter threat against home satellites; space-to-land attack weapons developed as new means of attacking important strategic military targets on land and water, and space-based anti-missile defense against ballistic missiles. The framework of a kinetic orbit weapon system is described with reference to a diagram and six key technologies are described, namely "kinetic interceptor/space-based kinetic intercepting missile technology," "precision detection, tracking and terminal guidance technology," "space combat platform general technology and platform wartime monitor and control technology," "space combat command and control technology," "space target monitoring, detection and tracking technology," and "technology for advanced carriers capable of fast and flexible launches."

The paper calls for continued monitoring of the new development of kinetic orbit weapons outside China, asserting that "kinetic orbit weapons will play a vital role in information, space and missile warfare." [Beijing *Xiandai Fangyu Jishu* in Chinese -- "*Modern Defence Technology*," bimonthly periodical, managed by CASIC, sponsored by Beijing Institute of Electronic System Engineering in cooperation with the Graduate School of the Second Research Academy of CASIC, and featuring academic studies and technical reports on air and space defense systems and weapons; missile technology; navigation, guidance, and control; command control and communication; detection and tracking technology; and simulation technology

4 "**Error Analysis of Orbit-transferring Velocity Increment on KKV in** Space" -- This article from the 2004, 3rd issue of *Zhuangbei Zhihui Jishu Xueyuan Xuebao* [*Journal of the Academy of Equipment Command & Technology*] by authors Ning Ziwen of the Academy of Equipment Command & Technology, Postgraduate Department and Yu Xiaohong of the Academy of Equipment Command & Technology, Department of Test Commanding, sets up a mathematic model based on the sensitivity of divert velocity increment of KKV in space, showing the effect of velocity increments error on hit precision by means of the basic result of Homan transfer orbit. It is seen that, "when the target orbit altitude and the velocity increment error are constant, the hit error caused by the velocity increment error when the space-based KKV is launched is decreased as a function of the increase in the velocity increment." Thus "one way of improving the hit precision of the space-based KKV is to provide a larger velocity increment to improve its divert ability," and thus "zero miss distance" can be achieved.

5 "**Design of Variable Structure Automatic Pilot for KKV**" -- This article from the 2004, 2nd issue of *Hangtian Kongzhi* [*Aerospace Control*] by author Huang Wanwei of Beijing Aerospace Automatic Control Institute, introduces with reference to a diagram the loop constituents and the dynamic model of the automatic pilot for KKV. It focuses on the variable structure control law in the design for the automatic pilot for KKV, and mathematical simulation is carried out. The simulation results show that the variable structure automatic pilot for KKV "is fast and has high attitude control accuracy," which satisfies the KKV requirements for attitude control. "The variable structure control is simple, easy to realize and has good engineering application prospects." [Beijing *Hangtian Kongzhi* in Chinese -- "*Aerospace Control*," bimonthly periodical, sponsored by the Beijing Aerospace Automatic Control Institute in cooperation with the Beijing Institute of Control Engineering and the Shanghai Electro-Mechanical Engineering Institute and featuring academic studies and technical reports on modern control theory and application; guidance navigation and control technology of missiles, launch vehicles, and spacecraft; computer technology and application; test launch and control technology; and other topics

6 "**An Investigation of a Maneuvering Long-Range Warhead's Capability to Break Through the Antimissile System**" -- This article from the 2003, 3rd issue of *Feixing Lixue* [*Flight Dynamics*] by authors He Zhengchun of Northeastern Polytechnic University, College of Astronautics and He Kaifeng of China Aerodynamics Research and Development Center, says that the Gulf wars marked the application stage of a new generation of antimissile defense systems. However, due to the technical difficulties and large investment involved, at present, "the best means of maintaining military deterrence for China is to develop the technology for missiles to break through a defense system." Following a brief survey of the missile defense systems abroad, it is noted that the US LEAP and THAAD and the kinetic interceptors based on these defense systems present a real threat to intercontinental missiles. An analysis of the overload necessary for a successful interception by the above type interceptors is therefore carried out. The results of the analysis show that "maneuvering a warhead, especially in the normal direction, can greatly increase its ability to break through an antimissile system." There are two ways of providing the divert power system necessary for maneuvering the warhead, one by adding a thruster and the other by using a divert propulsion system. The study says, meanwhile maneuvering the warhead "has the potential of further improving the hit precision of the warhead." "*Flight Dynamics,*" a quarterly technical journal published by COSTIND 7210 Flight Dynamics Group and the China Academy of Flight Experiment.

7 "**Preliminary Discussion on Solid Propellant Kinetic Kill Vehicle**" -- This article from the 2002, 4th issue of *Guti Hujian Jishu* [*Journal of Solid Rocket Technology*] by authors Zhang Hongan, Ye Dingyou, and Guo Peng of the 41st Institute of the Fourth Academy of CASC, introduces the significance and objectives of research on solid propellant KKV. It describes the basic composition of KKV, including its detection, guidance and power control equipment. The study explains the state of research and application abroad with a list of the major developments in the last ten years. It discusses two schemes of thrust vector control system for KKV dynamic control device, for example, three axis stability and direct applied force thrust vector control systems. It describes miniaturized KKV as the "key" to the development of kinetic energy weapons and "high performance solid propellants, new materials, and so on," as the key problems waiting further study

8 "**Terminal Guidance Analysis of Extra-Atmospheric Kinetic Kill Vehicle**" -- This paper from the 2002, 1st issue of *Feixing Lixue* [*Flight Dynamics*] by authors Cheng Fengzhou, Wang Ziming, and Chen Shilu of Northeastern Polytechnic University, College of Astronautics, examines terminal guidance of extra-atmospheric KKVs. It establishes the terminal guidance six-degree-of-freedom and dynamics models of the interceptor. It also studies the thrust performance and control model with trajectory control and altitude control, and the concept of appended proportional navigation law. It carries out the simulation of the terminal guidance procedure and analyzes some factors that affect the miss distance quantity. Simulation results show: 1.) the miss distance is sensitive to the initial conditions of the terminal guidance so that "the initial sight angle rate and the initial forward angel of the interceptor should be limited to a small range" to prevent "the required overload from surpassing the usable overload, resulting in a miss"; 2.) "When the target maneuvering speed is great, the interceptor may fail to hit the target because its usable overload is too small to satisfy the guidance requirements"; and 3.) "The initial deviation can be restricted to a certain extent by the attitude controller," but "cannot be completely eliminated.

9 "**Design and Realization of Terminal Guidance's Method for Kinetic Energy Interceptor at High Altitude**" -- This article from the 2001, 2nd issue of *Xiandai Fangyu Jishu* [*Modern Defence Technology*] by authors Zhang Yasheng of the Institute of Command and Technology, Department of Test Commanding, and Cheng Guocai and Chen Kejun of the National University of Defense Technology, Department of Automatic Control, proposes an effective guidance method for kinetic energy interceptor's terminal guidance that allows direct collision of the interceptor with its target by "restrained of sight of

line turn rate" guidance. Based on the engine of the interceptor, which is characterized as having constant thrust, multiple starts and impulse operational states, "an on/off switch control method is adopted using the curve determined by the proportional guidance as the on-switching curve and the value related to the sensitivity of the guide as the off-switching curve, the line of sight is restricted between the two curves so that the rate of turn is suppressed." The whole terminal guidance phase is divided into three sections -- rough control, careful control, and read-second -- where the engine operates using rated constant thrust and impulse for the first two sections, respectively, and an additional on-switch curve is designed for the read-second section to allow alternate on and off of the impulse engine, as in a game of "Go." The article says simulation using the model and design of the method proves its validity

 # 10 "Divert and Altitude Control System for a Kinetic Kill Vehicle Using Solid Propellant" -- This article from the 2001, 2nd Issue of *Feihang Daodan* [*Winged Missiles Journal*] by authors Zhang Dexiong and Wang Zhaobin of CASIC, 407th Institute, Fourth Division, briefly describes the solid propellant divert and attitude control engines of KKVs in the US defense system for intercepting missiles. Comparisons of the key technologies, the advantages and drawbacks are made with reference to figures and tables among MMA, ERINT, and SWARM, and the DACS of LEAP, the Standard-3 anti-missile system, and MEDUSA. It is concluded that the solid propellant DACS of KKV "will inevitably play a larger role" because, compared to liquid propellant system, it has "simple construction and good safety, is easy to store for long period of time and easy to maintain. It allows reduction in mass of the propulsion system and limited interference with attitude control. It reduces the overall cost of the missile and satisfies the safety requirements for "nonsensitive ammunition" by the US Navy and Air Force. [Beijing *Feihang Daodan* in Chinese -- "*Winged Missiles Journal*," monthly periodical published by China Aerospace Science and Industry Corporation (CASIC), Third Academy, 310th Research Institute and featuring reports on world and Chinese technologies on missiles, unmanned aerial vehicles, and related weapons systems.

Satellite Attacks On Earth Targets [2005][32]

[33]"The greatest advantage of a space-based ground attack weapon system is its high speed and short reentry time. It is extremely difficult for the enemy to intercept such a weapon. The war capsule is going to reenter in a ballistic mode. As a reference, an analysis was performed on the simulation of the ballistic reentry of a war capsule by using standard trajectory guidance. From the results, it is found that the standard trajectory method can be easily influenced by the initial errors upon reentry. It cannot accurately guide the war capsule to its targeted point of impact. In this paper, a combination of standard trajectory guidance and point of impact prediction guidance was used to simulate the guidance of a war capsule during its ballistic reentry in order to develop a better guidance algorithm. This work should provide a basis for the design of a better war capsule and its guidance system, as well as for its engineering application.

In theory, it can deal with a wider range of initial conditions with a higher degree of accuracy. Nevertheless, it requires a great deal of computation. Furthermore, its guidance law is far more complex. Hence, the onboard computer must have faster processing speed and larger storage capacity. It requires a more powerful high performance computer on board. In order to minimize the initial error, it is preferable to launch the war capsule at a larger angle of reentry. The guidance algorithm will produce a better effect and the point of impact will be more accurate."

---

[33] Zhanshu Daodan Kongzhi Jishu in Chinese 01 Sep 05

R&D on Future Beam Weapons for ASAT Missions

Since at least 1990, dozens of Chinese authors have described R&D on beam weapons in various technical journals. None has ever stated explicitly that China's leaders have actually authorized production and deployment of beam weapons. Rather, the authors report on finite research projects under way that could someday be part of a Chinese ASAT program. After China proposed a ban that would cover these types of beam weapons at the UN Conference on Disarmament in Geneva in 2002, the articles on progress in R&D continued to appear in scientific journals. Obviously, the Chinese technical press is controlled, and if someone advocated a politically taboo policy such as independence for Taiwan or Tibet, that author would suffer serious consequences, and not eve be allowed to publish. So these articles may be limited to revealing only that china is interested and active in potential development someday – perhaps after the US weaponizes space first.[34] It is also at least possible that China has already decided to acquire and then deploy beam weapons – which would be difficult for another nation to detect. If so, these articles could be seen in a different light and interpreted as progress reports on an authorized [but not fully developed] space weapons system. Open source literature cannot determine this kind of issue.

Eight years ago, the Defense Department began to warn in the 1998 Report to Congress on PRC Military Capabilities that "China already may possess the capability to damage, under specific conditions, optical sensors on satellites that are very vulnerable to damage by lasers. However, given China's current interest in laser technology, it is reasonable to assume that Beijing would develop a weapon that could destroy satellites in the future."

Beam weapons articles are not written by just a few speculative amateurs, as some US scholars have implied. Mark Stokes in 1999 estimated that 10,000 people, including approximately 3,000 engineers, in 300 organizations are involved in China's laser program, and that almost 40 percent of China's laser R&D is for military purposes. Lasers to be used for ASAT weapons need adaptive optics to penetrate the atmosphere, an area where China has sought foreign assistance.[35]

The China Aerospace Corporation (CASC) is among the strongest advocates for an anti-satellite (ASAT) development program,[36] with authors there often arguing that an ASAT capability is needed to deter potential adversaries from attacking China's own satellites. Authors imply that research (yuxian yanjiu) on ASATs has been carried out since the 1980s, at least partly funded under the 863 Program for High Technology Development.

CASC researchers, primarily concentrated within the Second Academy, are leading China's R&D of counterspace systems. Several articles have appeared in the Second Academy's journal, Systems Engineering and Electronics, about problems in negating adversarial satellites.[37] The Harbin Institute of Technology and Beijing University of Astronautics and Aeronautics have carried out modeling of space intercept control and terminal guidance systems. One concept was the use of small solid motors for orbital

---

[34] US work in the field is discussed in David Shukman, *Tommorrow's War: The Threat of High-Technology Weapons*, New York: Harcourt Brace, 1996,

[35] One particular laser optics facility with which China cooperates is the AGAT R&D establishment in Belarus. Chi Haotian visited AGAT in early June 1997. See "Prime Minister Linh Meets Chinese Defense Minister," Moscow Interfax, June 3, 1997, in FBIS-SOV-97-154

[36] Mark A. Stokes, *China's Strategic Modernization: Implications for the United States*, Army War College, September 1999.

[37] Yang Qunfu and Liu Xiao'en, "Fanweixing Wuqi Xitong Fazhan Qianjing de Yanjiu" ("Study on the Developmental Prospects for ASAT Weapon Systems"), Hangtian Qingbao Yanjiu (Aerospace Information Research), March 1993. Third Academy assessed an air launched ASAT System, according to Stokes' 1999 study.

control stabilization. CASC authors in the Third Academy have assessed air launched ASAT missiles and called this approach the most inexpensive ASAT option.

Chinese aerospace analysts contrast the capabilities of ground-based high-powered lasers, able to degrade satellites including those in geosynchronous orbits, as an alternative in e to kinetic kill vehicles. As a part of its high-powered laser program, Chinese authors describe work on adaptive optics and deformable mirrors. Adaptive optics authors are based at the Shanghai Institute of Optics and Fine Mechanics and Anhui Institute of Optics and Fine Mechanics. CAEP's Institute of Applied Physics and Computational Mathematics (IAPCM) has supported the effort through modeling work on atmospheric effects on ground based high-powered laser weapons.[38]

Second Academy authors also evaluate High Power Microwave weapons in a counterspace role.[39]

Nor are beam weapons articles being written solely by scientists. Beam weapons are frequently mentioned in broad surveys by PLA officers on future space warfare. An important example is the discussion by Ping Fan and Li Qi, "A Theoretical Discussion of Several Matters Involved in the Development of Military Space Forces."[40] Ping and Li are from COSTIND's Command Technology Academy.

Recommendations about at least five types of beam weapons feature in these articles:

X-ray Laser. X-ray lasers, in principle, can destroy electrical circuitry, possibly trigger some types of munitions, and set off nuclear weapons. The preferred energy source is a small nuclear explosion. However, China, which claims certain aspects of its X-ray laser program to be the most advanced in the world, appears to be focusing on using high powered lasers to produce X-ray lasing..[41] China Academy of Engineering Physics (CAEP) is China's leading institute on the development of X-ray laser systems. At least one prototype X-ray driver, the Shenguang-1 device, was tested as early as 1988.[42]

Chemical Oxygen-Iodine Laser (COIL). Dalian Institute of Chemistry and Physics (DICP) is responsible for China's COIL development program, which they acknowledge
has the potential to be an effective DEW. COIL research in Dalian began in the early 1980s and was formally accepted as an 863 project in April 1991. Progress has been made into both pulsed and CW modes. Dalian scientists claim they are among the world's leaders in COIL research..

Laser Satellite Tracking. For more than a decade, China has used lasers to track satellites in space. Laser range finders are located at space observatories in Wuhan, Nanjing, Beijing, Kunming, Lintong, and Shanghai. Anhui Institute of Optics and Fine Mechanics play a large role in the development of these systems, as well as excimer lasers and the atmospheric effects on laser transmission. China's satellite laser

---

[38] "Methods for Investigating Near-Field Power in Ground-Based High Power Laser Weapon Testing," Zhongguo Jiguang (Chinese Journal of Lasers), December 1992, in JPRS-CST-93-008.

[39] . Li Hui and Wang Zibin, "Development of High Powered Microwave Weapons and Their Applications for Counterspace and Air Defense," Zhidao yu Yinxin, 1995 (1), pp. 3-15, in CAMA, 1995, Vol. 2, No. 3.

[40] Ping Fan and Li Qi, "A Theoretical Discussion of Several Matters Involved in the Development of Military Space Forces." Zhongguo Junshi Kexue (China Military Science), May 20, 1997, pp. 127-131

[41] . "China Scores Marked Results in Laser Technology Research," Jiefangjun Bao, February 13, 1996, in FBIS-CHI-96-038. Also see "ICF, X-ray Laser Experiments With LF-12 (Shenguang) Apparatus Described," Renmin Ribao, May 3, 1991, JPRS-CST-91-019

[42] . "Development of Flash X-ray Machines at CAEP," Qiang Jiguang Yu Lizishu, August 1991, JPRS-CST-92-001.

range finders, which have an accuracy of 3-4 centimeters, assist in real-time tracking for China's Launch and Tracking Control (CLTC).

Anti-Satellite Lasers. Chinese engineers have conducted at least theoretical research into the use of high powered lasers and other directed energy weapons against satellites and have closely studied U.S. and former Soviet ASAT systems, including the U.S. MIRACL, COIL, EMRLD projects, and former Soviet DEW systems at Sary Sagan.

Laser Radar. Chinese engineers strongly advocate the development of CO_2 laser radars (lidar), especially for countering a potential adversary's cruise missiles. Supported by the 863 Program, Anhui Institute of Optics and Fine Mechanics has developed one of China's first lidars, which has a maximum detection range of 50 kilometers. Other applications include GEO satellite tracking..

Part 3. Desirable Goals of a US-China Dialogue on Space Weapons

This survey of open source literature supports the USCC recommendation to Congress that the US executive branch should initiate a dialogue with China on space weapons issues. The content of such a dialogue is beyond the scope of this report. However, this survey suggests at least six broad areas in which the US could profitably exchange views with Chinese specialists. Prior to initiating such a strategic dialogue, these six areas would need careful thought.

- **Reducing Chinese Misperceptions of US Space Policy**

- **Increasing Chinese Transparency on Space Weapons**

- **Probing Chinese Interest in Verifiable Agreements**

- **Multilateral vs. Bilateral Approaches**

- **Economic Consequences of Use of Space Weapons**

- **Reconsideration of US High Tech Exports to China**

Part 4. Implications for US Policy

This survey of Chinese open-source literature on recommendations for the future development of antisatellite weapons raises a number of policy issues.

1. Possible US Countermeasures – Awareness, Assessing Damage, Forensics, Counter Strikes

One may usefully speculate what the military and economic consequences would be for the US if all thirty of these recommendations were actually funded and implemented by China. Of the thirty proposals, one set would be particularly challenging to US military vulnerabilities in a crisis. In each of their books, Chinese Colonels Li, Jia and Yuan all advocated **covert** deployment of a sophisticated antisatellite weapon system to be used against United States in a surprise manner without warning. The number of US satellites to be targeted and attacked was not specified by the three Chinese authors, but Colonel Yuan specified that China's future "shock and awe" attack must be devastating enough to deter any further American military action in a crisis and "bring the opponent to his knees." All three colonels reference the traditional concept of space attack as an "assassin's mace weapon" that is decisive in its use of surprise. Even a small attack could have major consequences. Chinese sources credit the United States with more than 400 satellites out of the approximately 800 satellites now currently active in space. Even a small scale antisatellite attack in a crisis against 50 US satellites [assuming a mix of targeted military reconnaissance, navigation satellites, and communication satellites] could have a catastrophic effect not only on US military forces, but of the US civilian economy. It is not clear from US open sources how rapidly--if at all--United States could launch "spare" satellites to replace a few dozen that had been incapacitated in orbit by a Chinese attack. US sources refer to many [very expensive] countermeasures such as maneuvering satellites in orbit to escape destruction, using constellations of small satellites, rapid replacement with spares, and even prompt counter strikes on the Chinese launchers. [43]

A second set of Chinese concepts proposed in these open source writings would also be particularly challenging. Many of the concepts recommended include both jamming and attacking ground stations, rather than the permanent destruct ruction of US satellites. In both cases, the Chinese authors imply the United States may lack the "forensic" ability to know which nation had neutralized US space systems through covert attack, jamming or destruction of ground stations by missile or Special Forces raids. The US Defense Department currently has put before Congress various proposals for enhancing situational awareness of space attack, but the ultimate approval of multiple-year funding is unknown.

2. Implications of Dialogues with These ASAT Authors

All of the articles cited in this study may be dismissed by Chinese diplomatic sources as mere idle speculation by various "maverick" authors. While that may be a convenient diplomatic position, we are forced to accept the studies and recommendations as valid considering that the authors are in positions of influence within Chinese military and technology hierarchies and are employed at Chinese research institutes some of which actually manufacture space, missile and electronic systems. It is important that the US establish with the Chinese the serious importance to which we assign this published, detailed advocacy of Chinese weaponization of space. It is likely that a persuasive dialogue will not be possible solely with Chinse diplomats [or other officials assigned to deal with foreigners] and that the most

---

[43] For a list of countermeasures, see "Space Systems Survivability,." Uri Ra'anan and Robert L Pfaltzgraff, Jr, eds., *International Security Dimensions of Space*, Hamden CT, Archon Books, 1984, pp 87-93.

effective course would be formay be useful for US representatives to meet directly with some or all of these authors for discussions at their government organizations. Access to ASAT specialists in China has been impossible in the DOD exchange programs in the past decade, according to some observers, because China prohibits ASAT experts from participating in the exchanges at all. The 3 NDU authors cited may never have visited the US, and, as started, seem unaware of the Congressional restrains on US space programs.

3. Detecting the Signatures of Future Chinese ASAT, impact of proposals on US policy decisions

An implication for the US intelligence community of these Chinese proposals would be the feasibility of identifying the developmental"signatures" of the recommended covert systems through normal intelligence collection. It may be difficult and probably impossible to detect the manufacturing and testing of many of the components that are proposed. The authors make clear in many of the recommendations that the acquisition of the systems and even their deployment are to be done covertly in a manner that cannot be detected by United States until the moment of their use by China in a crisis. Plasma attack, attacks on GPS, use of stealthy satellites, penetration and destruction of ground stations, jamming based on deceptive transmissions that imitate US signals, experimental units that can be converted in a crisis, ASATs fired from submarines -- all these concepts could potentially be concealed in advance of their use unless their signatures were anticipated. By definition, the Chinese government would deny the existence of such covert programs. Indeed, consideration must be given to the possibility that active duty colonels have been permitted to publish such proposals as an effort to influence US thinking regarding the potential vulnerabilities and lack of effectiveness of possible space based national missile defense components, thus discouraging their development and acquisition. Likewise, these proposals may have been allowed as a form of counterthreat against US first deployment of space weapons.

4. Concerns of Japan, India, European Union and Russia to Chinese ASAT

In terms of multilateral diplomacy and US alliances, one might ask whether other nations in addition to the United States have any concerns about these proposals and recommendations. Japan, but not India or Russia has expressed concern about China's lack of transparency in the military area that would presumably include the development of anti system antisatellite systems. The question would be whether China in the future may be the subject of pressure from the international community in addition to the United States.

5. Verification and On Site Inspections of an ASAT Agreement?

With respect to US arms control policy, some advocates propose that we re-think the question of refusal to negotiate or discuss the Chinese proposal to the UN conference on disarmament in Geneva on a non-verifiable agreement against weaponization in outer space. If such an agreement explicitly permitted American National missile defense and was verifiable with on-site inspection, it might merit negotiation. After all, China has accepted 100 visits by the inspection organization of the chemical weapons ban, so the precedent exists of China's accepting on-site inspections for international arms control agreements. Of course, the ban will be reciprocal so the United States would be compelled to accept inspections potentially of sensitive facilities under the control the national reconnaissance organization which manufactures highly classified US satellites and space systems.

6. Inference of Chinese Determinations of US Space Weapons activities and plans

With regard to future Sino-American exchanges and dialogue, one might ask what precisely are the catalysts or red lines that China seems to be suggesting will compel it to initiate the acquisition and deployment of space-based systems including antisatellite weapons. One school of thought has been that the United States national missile defense system threatens China's nuclear deterrent. This may be why antisatellite systems can be justified. Another view may be that the United States has in China's view already crossed the red line compelling a Chinese decision to develop antisatellite weapons, by refusing to discuss the Chinese arms-control offer to ban space weapons and by America's currently funded missile defense programs. This issue is significant because an effort to engage China in a dialogue on space weapons would be futile and even naïve if the decision has already has been made by Chinese leaders because of their misperceptions of existing US policies and programs.

7. China's Proposed Space Weapons Ban and Current US Missile Defenses

In terms of understanding Chinese motives for a proposal in 2002 for a space weapons ban, that is, a decade after Chinese authors first recommended ASAT development, it is useful to keep in mind the relevant chronology. The American arms-control community has actively advocated a ban on space weapons systems since at least 1999, as can be seen in the appendix [Bibliography on Space Arms Control]. It seems possible therefore that China's proposal in Geneva in 2002 may have been stimulated by three or more years of observing US arms-control community proposals for space weapons bans. These US advocates had concerns about space weaponization that were in fact closely linked to their opposition to any US missile defense. The US arms control advocates, like the Chinese, also vehemently opposed any national missile defense and withdrawal from the Anti Ballistic Missile Treaty. They even opposed the proposal of Senator Sam Nunn over a decade ago for GPALS, "global protection against accidental launched missiles system," which envisioned about 100 ground-based interceptors. The current missile Defense agency description of US national missile Defense implies implicitly that 20 ground-based interceptors is the near-term ceiling. As early as 1999, Richard Garwin published his opposition to such missile defense and warned against an arms race in space. China may have decided to ally itself tactically with these American advocates in the US policy debate on missile defense by adopting their ideas against weaponization of space – even though Chinese military and technical specialists and been advocating antisatellite weapons for many years.

If this hypothesis is correct, it helps to explain why China permitted the publication of three rather provocative books in 2001, 2002, and 2005 by military officers' with their proposals for covert deployment of antisatellite weapons directed at US assets. The publication of these books and other explicit recommendations advocating future antisatellite programs may have been authorized as part of a larger design to influence the US policy debate in the Congress and the media. One goal would be to oppose the extensive proposal by Senator Sam Nunn for a national missile defense system of 100 interceptors. If China essentially is threatening to deploy a robust ASAT system in the decade or two ahead, it makes a powerful case against even the current modest 20 interceptor system of in the present program.

8. Space-related Export Controls and Further Restrictions on Deemed Exports

There are substantial export control issues involved in any US decision to oppose or impede China's potential acquisition of antisatellite systems. We might ask whether more restrictive technology transfers on China could head off Chinese development of some or all of the antisatellite systems listed in the proposals identified in open sources. For example, nanotechnology laminated surfaces, miniature rocket motors; quick launch space vehicle propulsion, and directed energy technology (especially advance performance lasers), precision space guidance systems, and various bilateral technology exchanges such as the current program of the National Science Foundation for cooperation in remote sensing will become areas to examine for additional technology transfer restrictions. It would be a major project to identify and design new export controls on US technologies related to anti- satellite weapons acquisition and deployment.

Many other issues involving space technology transfer to China fall within the purview of the broader issues to be assessed by the newly created "Deemed Exports Advisory Commission." In 2004, the Department of Commerce failed to initiate a policy proposal to consider the transfer of knowledge inside United States as a "deemed export" (requiring an export license). According to a then-member of the Deemed Exports Advisory Commission, Robert Gates in interview with Defense News in October 15, 2006, Cold War standards may not be sufficient any more to protect technology.

9. PACOM and STRATCOM Role in Educating the PLA on Consequences of China's Use of ASAT

9. The US Department of Defense has extensive exchange programs in its "theater engagement plans" and may wish to play a greater role in deterring Chinese development of space weapons. Both Strategic Command and Pacific Command may wish to consider in their discussions on track one and track 1.5 whether to include information about the consequences of an attack on US military satellites in a crisis as part of their routine presentations on US defense policy and strategy to the Chinese.

10. Recommendations in Open Sources vs. China's Real Intentions

It is difficult to rely on Chinese open source literature as the sole source for a persuasive strategic warning that vulnerable US military command, communications and sensitive national intelligence systems may all be in jeopardy in the decade ahead. The concern might be called the "methodology for military analysis." On one side, a number of US specialists on Chinese military affairs have been erecting a filter over the past decade that tends to belittle any Chinese open source writings. These specialists assert that a military capability must go through a long process of development before it can be considered a credible force. Antisatellite weapons would need to be researched, designed, manufactured, tested, deployed, and then have a series of operational exercises, and a clear doctrine would have to be written and disseminated, not to mention the absolute requirement for the drafting and exercising of operational plans for an antisatellite attack. These specialists add to this long list of requirements another insurmountable challenge – mere colonels at Chinese defense universities and mere aerospace engineers or other specialists in China aerospace organizations do not have the authority required to authorize and execute an anti-satellite or space weapons program. Only China's President and the CCP Politburo and Central Military Commission has such authority, and none of those institutions has issued any recommendations to develop such weapons.

On the other side stands the fascinating work of several US historians and political scientists on the causes of war, and on the sources of intelligence failure. Thomas Mahnken argues that in many cases it has proved to be impossible for intelligence analysts to identify new weapons and operational concepts unless there own armed forces already such capabilities. Neither the Nazi German blitzkrieg nor the Japanese tactics at Pearl Harbor in 1941 were "recognized" as patterns in advance in spite of available evidence. In related studies, MIT Professor Steven Van Evera has concluded that "first move advantage" can be a cause of war. In his new book from Harvard University Press, Dominic Johnston asserts that overconfidence in one's own [untested] military forces has also been a common cause of war in history.

Robert Jervis has warned that some types of war – nuclear warfare in particular – has never happened, so that it is unrealistic to expect to know how it may start, continue, escalate or terminate. Space warfare has never happened. No one can really know what the shape of a Chinese preemptive attack on US satellites might be like, or what the US response might be. US studies of China's prior use of force in 1950, 1962, 1969 and 1979 have all conclude that the Chinese place high value on surprising the opponent – even when Beijing was motivated by entirely "defensive" Chinese concerns.

If we know little about how space warfare may unfold because it has never happened, is it wise to dismiss the probative value of Chinese open source recommendations on the grounds that no one has yet seen China start to manufacture, test, exercise, and write doctrine for real space weapons? It would seem that open source materials containing recommendations for future ASAT concepts deserve more attention than to be completely dismissed, just as they cannot be considered to be completely definitive.

At a minimum, these writings suggest the need for a more assertive US engagement effort with the authors and their organizations. At a maximum, these writings suggest a major misperception by at least the authors and possible the Chinese leadership that US efforts to "weaponize space" are decades away, if the US Congress ever permits such efforts at all.

These Chinese authors could benefit from studies such as Dwayne A. Day's that conclude that "one could assemble a pretty neat comic book containing all of these over-ambitious unaffordable or just plain unnecessary military space weapons system that Air Force generals have insisted were vital….this disconnect between the speechmakers and the budgeters and operators is not something the general media understands when it reports about military space [plans]."[44]

---

[44] Dwyane .A Day, "General Power vs. Chicken Little," *Spaceflight*,May 23, 2005.

Documentary Appendix

Bibliography of Chinese Sources

Military Journals with Little Space Content

These standard military journals generally do <u>not</u> contain articles on ASATs or space warfare.

Logistics Studies Houqin Xueshu 后勤学术

Military Studies Junshi Xueshu 军事学术

Armament Equipment Technology Junxie Zhuangbei Jishu 军械装备技术

NDU Journal Guofang Daxue Xuebao 国防大学学报

Army Finance Jundui Caiwu 军队财务

Military-Use Vehicles Junyong Qiche 军用汽车

Naval Studies Research Haijun Xueshu Yanjiu 海军学术研究

Military Economics Research Junshi Jingji Yanjiu 军事经济研究

Modern Military Branches Xiandai Bingzhong 现代兵种

Air Force Logistics Research Kongjun Houqin Yanjiu 空军后勤研究

Command Journal Zhihui Xuebao 指挥学报

Atillery Studies Magazine Paoxue Zazhi 炮学杂志

China Military Education Zhongguo Junshi Jiaoyu 中国军事教育

China Military Science Zhongguo Junshi Kexue 中国军事科学

Military Finance Junshi Caiwu 军事财务

Modern Military Xiandai Junshi 现代军事 1

Nanjing Logistics Nanjing Houqing 南京后勤

National Defense Journal Guofang Tongbao 国防通报

List of 80 Chinese Space Journals & Websites

Chinese media covering missile and space issues can be divided into two basic categories: 1) specialized news magazines, papers, and websites and 2) science and technology journals, both in hardcopy and online.   Many media of both categories are sponsored by one of two major state-owned enterprises: China Aerospace Science and Technology Corporation (CASC) and China Aerospace Science and Industry Corporation (CASIC).   Other sponsors include industry associations under the China Association for Science and Technology.

The specialized news media sometimes carry general reports on developments in China's military but more often dwell on civilian programs, such as the manned space program.   All media are controlled by the government and do not stray outside certain political and security bounds.

The following list of publications is limited to those with information on Chinese missiles and space systems.   The list is not necessarily exhaustive but represents the majority of openly available media on this topic.

1. China Space News

Zhongguo Hangtian Bao started publication on 1 January 1986.   Sponsored jointly by the China Aerospace Science and Technology Corporation (CASC) and the China Aerospace Science and Industry Corporation (CASIC), it is one of the major national newspapers in China.   It carries news on aerospace events, popular astronautic science knowledge, anecdotes of famous aerospace individuals, space exploration, and hot spots in society so on.   It is published biweekly, with its front page designated for Important News, second page for Comprehensive News, third page for Economics Hot Line, fourth page for Popular Science Salon, and so on.   Its online version can be found at www.china-spacenews.com.

2. Aerospace China
www.spacechina.com

Zhongguo Hangtian started publication in 1987.   It is sponsored by CASC's China National Aerospace Information Center with the aim of becoming a bridge and link of exchange between aerospace circles at home and abroad.   The main contents of the journal are as follows: China Report, Aerospace Industry and National Economy, Aerospace Policy and Management, Aerospace Systems and Technology, Space Exploration, Missiles and Other Weapon Systems, and so on.

3. Aerospace Knowledge

Hangkong Zhishi is a monthly magazine sponsored by the Chinese Society of Aeronautics and Astronautics and managed by the China Association of Science and Technology.   The magazine reports on a wide variety of aerospace topics, including domestic and international, civilian and military, air and space.

4. Space International

Guoji Taikong started publication in 1979 and is sponsored by Beijing Space Scientific and Technological Information Institute to introduce the newest accomplishment in China's aerospace sector and report the new trends in aerospace activities both at home and abroad.   The main contents of the journal are as follows: China Space, Popular and Focal Topics, Space Tour, Star Interview, Manned Space Flight, Flight Malfunction, Space Exploration, Space File, and so on.   The Internet address of the journal is www.cast.com.cn.

5. Space exploration

Taikong Tansuo, a monthly originally known as Aerospace, started publication in 1981 and is sponsored by the China Aerospace Society.   Issued both at home and abroad, it claims it is the only authoritative periodical for popular space science in China, integrating knowledge, readability, practicability, and interest.   The journal aims to popularize space knowledge, publicize China aerospace, and explore the secrets of outer space.   It has special columns of Hot and Focal Spot, New Routes to Space, Universe Secrets, Most Advanced Weapons, Manned Space Flight, and so on.

6. Aerospace World

Shijie Hangkong Hangtian Bolan is a large-scale semimonthly military journal.   It started publication in 1998 and is sponsored by CASC's China National Aerospace Information Center.   The journal has an exclusive use license for the Hong Kong based journal entitled Junshi Jia [Militarist] in Mainland China. The main contents of Shijie Hangkong Hangtian Bolan A (published in the first half of each month) are as follows: World Military News, Militarist Observatory, Insider's Information on Military and Weapon Equipment, Foreign Commentary, Taiwan Military Trends, Aeronautic and Astronautic Shows, Famous Weapon Museums, and so on.   The main contents of Shijie Hangkong Hangtian Bolan B (published in the second half of each month) are as follows: Military Report, China's Military Strength, Elite Strategy, Weapon Ranking, Green Club, and so on.   Its Internet address is www.spacechina.com.

7. China National Space Administration
www.cnsa.gov.cn/index.asp

The website of the China National Space Administration has a news section called Comprehensive Reports, carrying domestic and international aerospace news reposted from other news sites.   It has special columns on Aerospace and Politics, Space Commercialization, Space Station, Space Weapons, Space Shuttles, Outer Space, International Cooperation, Delivery and Propulsion Technology, Satellites and Application, Aerospace Programs, and Launch Activities.

8. Commission of Science Technology and Industry for National Defense
www.costind.gov.cn/htm/kjcg/zhuanhua.asp

The website of the Commission of Science Technology and Industry for National Defense has the section Scientific Accomplishments and Exchange.   Within this section, there is a special column entitled Aerospace Scientific Accomplishments.   The column provides a list of aerospace technological accomplishments that can be commercialized for the national economic development.

9. Newsletter of the Ministry of S&T
www.most.gov.cn/English/newletter/newsletter2004.htm

The website of the Chinese Ministry of Science and Technology has the special section S&T Newsletter that carries news on the development of science and technology in China, including aerospace events. The first article in issue No. 357 dated 10 February 2004, for example, is entitled Asia-Pacific Space Cooperation.

10. China Aerospace Science & Technology Corporation
www.spacechina.com/espace/

The website of the China Aerospace Science and Technology Corporation, hosted by the National Aerospace Information Center, has the section News & Information that carries articles on domestic aerospace events reposted from other news sites.   There is also a section called Products, which carries news on the company's products, such as launch vehicles, man-made satellites and so on.   Another section called Launch Record provides a list of the company's launch activities.

11. Chinese Academy of Space Technology (CAST)
www.cast.cn/

The website of the Chinese Academy of Space Technology has a News section, which is further divided into the three subsections of National News, Industry News, and International News, reporting domestic and international aerospace events reposted from other news sites.   It also has other sections called Products, Research Fields, International Cooperation, and so on.

12. China Academy of Launch Vehicle Technology (CALT)
www.calt.com/news/

The website of the China Academy of Launch Vehicle Technology (CALT) has a news section, mostly articles on domestic and international aerospace events reposted from other news sites.   There is also a section carrying news on events within the academy.

13. China Great Wall Industry Corp.
www.cgwic.com.cn/chinese/application/index.html

According to its website, the China Great Wall Industry Corp. has been acting as the tie and bridge between the Chinese and global space community.   Its website has special sections for   What's New, Launch Services, Satellites and Application, and Trade and Services.

14. Shanghai Academy of Spaceflight Technology
www.sast.org/default1.htm

The website of the Shanghai Academy of Spaceflight Technology has three news sections called Shanghai Aerospace, China Aerospace, and International Aerospace containing mostly articles on domestic and international aerospace events reposted from other news sites.   There is also a section called Shanghai Aerospace Newsflash carrying news updates on aerospace events within China and worldwide.

15. Satellite Applications

Weixing Yingyong started publication in June 1993.   Jointly sponsored by the Commission of Science Technology and Industry for National Defense, the PLA General Armament Department (GAD), and CASC, it is a quarterly journal with restricted distribution.   As an interdisciplinary and comprehensive publication, the journal extensively covers research work, practical accomplishments, technological progress, system development, and so on in the field of satellite applications.   It also carries the current international accomplishments and development trends in satellite applications.

16. Infrared and Laser Engineering

17. Hongwai yu Jiguang Gongcheng, a bimonthly Chinese edition with English abstracts, is sponsored by CASC.   As a key journal in the fields of   telecommunications and radio engineering, the journal advertises itself as the best way to know IR & Laser technology progress in the China aerospace industry.   It focuses on applications of infrared and laser technology in space science, especially in the research and design of satellites and missile weapon systems.   New methods and the results of experiments, new techniques and materials, and new achievements in   applications of infrared and laser technology in civil industry are also introduced in its technical reports and research papers.   With the latest updates   on theories and practices, the journal shows the current status and development of infrared and laser technology in China.

Aerospace Technology & Civilian Products

18. Hangtian Jishu yu Minpin, a monthly, is sponsored by CASC's Institute for Astronautics Information.   It is a comprehensive and informative technical magazine circulated to readers at home and abroad.   It mainly covers the results of space R&D, civilian products, bidding projects, management experiences, technical innovations made by domestic and foreign related organizations, related policies and regulations, projects of technical transfer, and new technologies and products.   It also makes analyses on the technical market and gives suggestions on countermeasures.   The journal aims to serve those who are engaged in technical research, product development, and management.

19. Computer Engineering and Design

Jisuanji Gongcheng yu Sheji, a bimonthly, is sponsored by the Beijing Computer Technology and Applications Institute, under CASC.   It is a scientific journal carrying articles on various kinds of computers and computer systems, including reports, surveys and reviews on researching, analyzing, designing, and developing computers and applications.   The journal is helpful to those who are engaged in the work of scientific research, teaching, development, application, consultant services, and information processing.

20. Aerospace Control

Hangtian Kongzhi started publication in 1983 and is sponsored by the Beijing Aeropace Automatic Control Institute.   It is a technical journal covering the technological development standard at home and abroad in the fields of both navigation guidance and control.   The journal has the following major special columns: Missiles, Launch Vehicle Guidance and Control Technology, Spacecraft Navigation Guidance, Navigation and Control Technology, Simulation Technology, and so on.   The Internet address of the journal is htkz.chinajournal.net.cn.

21. Journal of Astronautic Metrology and Measurement

Yuhang Jice Jishu started publication in 1981 and is sponsored jointly by CASC's 102 Institute and 203 Institute.   It mainly covers the design of measurement standards for length, heat, mechanics, radio, time frequency, electromagnetics, chemistry, and optics.   It also covers development and manufacturing, measurement test technology, diagnostic maintenance technology of both instruments and meters, error analysis, data processing technology, and so on.

22. Journal of Propulsion Technology

Tuijin Jishu, a bimonthly, first published in 1980 and has been available abroad since 1988.   Sponsored by Beijing Power Generating Machinery Institute and CASC, it is one of the key scientific journals in China and reflects the research and development status of the propulsion systems for missiles and space vehicles in China.   It mainly carries thesis, research papers, and reports on design, test, manufacture, and applications of propulsion systems for missiles, launch vehicles, and spacecraft.   It also covers the related spin-offs of propulsion technology.   The journal aims to serve scientists, engineers, teachers, students, and decision makers engaged in the research and development of missiles and space vehicle propulsion. It is a window through which China exchanges space propulsion technology information with the rest of the world.

Computer Simulation

23. Jisuanji Fangzhen is a comprehensive quarterly journal, managed by CASC, sponsored by the Editorial Office of Computer Simulation, and under the editing and publishing control of Beijing KW System Integrated Co., Ltd.   The journal provides information on advanced technology and methodology in the field of computer simulation in China.   Topics in the journal include modeling, algorithms, experimental methods, virtual reality, artificial intelligence, and so on.

China Astronautics and Missilery Abstracts

24. Zhongguo Daodan yu Hangtian Wenzhai is a bimonthly and bilingual (Chinese/English) journal sponsored by CASC's Institute for Astronautics Information.   As the only reference journal on aerospace and rockets in China, it exhaustively cites the latest aerospace, missile, and defense related documents produced in China.   A CD-ROM version of China Aerospace Database is also available. The CD-ROM contains more than 250,000 records dating back to 1985 (Chinese edition) or 15,000 records dating back to 1994 (English edition).

China Military and Civilian Use Technology and Products

25. Junmin Liangyong Jishu yu Chanpin started publication in 1988.   It is sponsored by CASC's China National Aerospace Information Center to track and report trends in both developments and markets in the fields of military and civilian technologies.   The main contents of the journal are as follows: Special Report, Industrial Trends, Astronautics and Aeronautics, Ships, Automobiles and Vehicles, Computers and Networks, Communications, Industrial Interview, and Classic Case.   Its Internet address is www.chinatoptech.com.

Aerospace Industry Management

26. Hangtian Gongye Guanli started publication in 1983.   It is sponsored by CASC's China National Aerospace Information Center to introduce and review experiences, lessons, problems, and the corresponding solutions relating to R&D, production, and management in the field of national defense industry both at home and abroad.   The main contents of the journal are as follows: Study and Discussion, Management and Practice, Industrial Trends, Industrial Informatization, Industrial Culture, Management Review, Lesson, and Case Analysis.

Scientific Policy Decision

27. Kexue Juece started publication in 1994.   It is sponsored jointly by China Social Economic Systems

Analysis Research Association, CASC's 710 Institute, and the International Information Institute of China. The main contents of the journal are as follows: Development Forum, Exclusive Interview, Finance and Bonds, International Observation, Regional Economy, Commodity Market, High Education, Typical Case, International Security, Science and Technology, Industrial Culture, Decision Debate, and so on.

Aerospace Standardization

28. Hangtian Biaozhunhua is a comprehensive scientific and technological periodical covering both space high-tech accomplishments and the related application standardization. The journal started publication in 1983 and is sponsored by CASC's China Institute of Space Standardization. The main contents of the journal are as follows: Policy, Goals and Tasks, Study and Discussion, Standard Introduction and Implementation, Standardization in Model Research, Industrial Standardization, Foreign Standardization, and so on. The Internet address of the journal is htbh.chinajournal.net.cn.

Quality and Reliability

29. hiliang yu Kekaoxing is a comprehensive scientific and technological periodical integrating guidance, academics, practicability, popularity, and interest. It started publication in 1986 and is sponsored jointly by China Quality Society of Space and CASC's 708 Institute. The main contents of the journal are as follows: Policy and Strategy, Theory and Method, Exclusive Interview, Quality Culture, Practical Experience, Software Engineering, Foreign Space Information, and so on. The Internet address of the journal is www.ht708.com.cn.

Chinese Space Science and Technology

30. Zhongguo Kongjian Kexue Jishu started publication in 1981 and is sponsored by China Academy of Space Technology. It covers various aspects in the field of space science and technology of China such as the corresponding research accomplishments, technological accomplishments, and academic knowledge. The main contents of the journal are as follows: Research and Exploration, Special Subject Discussion, and Technology Exchange. The Internet address of the journal is zgkj.chinajournal.net.cn.

Journal of Telemetry, Tracking, and Command

31. Yaoce Yaokong started publication in 1976 and is sponsored by CASC's 704 Institute. It covers new development results in the field of remote measurement and control technologies and reports theoretical and applied research results of the same field as well as research results on both related systems and products. The main contents of the journal are as follows: Scientific Paper and Technical Report, Comprehensive Review and Commentary, Scientific Discussion, New Technology Introduction, Promising Small Technology Introduction, Scientific and Technological Trend, Special Topic Lecture and Book Review.

Cryogenic Engineering

32. Diwen Gongcheng started publication in 1979. It is sponsored by CASC's 101 Institute and covers mainly scientific papers and research reports in the following areas: Cryogenic Technology, Gas Liquidation and Separation Technology, Liquefied Gas Storage Technology, Cryogenic Isolation Technology, Cryogenic Sealing and Related Materials, Cryogenic Parameter Measurement Technology, Cryogenic Safety Technology, Application of Cryogenic Technology in Aerospace Engineering Research,

and so on.

Vacuum and Cryogenics

33. Zhenkong Diwen started publication in 1982, and is sponsored by CASC's 510 Institute.   The journal introduces and deals with development trends, new equipment, new processes, new materials, and new approaches.   It also reflects applications and developments in both modern vacuum and cryogenic sciences and technologies.   The journal has the following major columns: Comprehensive Review, Research Report, Knowledge and Advancement, Market Information, and so on.

Space Electronic Technology

34. Kongjian Dianzi Jishu started publication in 1971 and is sponsored by the Xi'an Space Radio Technology Institute. It aims to exchange space electronic technology, train young technical personnel, refresh the academic research environment, and promote aerospace development.   The journal has the following major columns: Review and Research, Technical Report, Design and Measurement, New Technology and Process, Information and Trends, and so on.

Microelectronics and Computers

35. Weidianzixue yu Jisuanji started publication in 1972 and is sponsored by CASC's 771 Institute.   It is a Chinese language multidisciplinary, comprehensive, vocational core scientific and technological periodical in China.   The journal mainly publishes papers in the following areas: Microelectronic Process and Device, Computer Theory and Application, Networks and Communications, Software and Algorithms, and so on.

Missiles and Space Vehicles

36. Daodan yu Hangtian Yunzai Jishu started publication in 1972 and is sponsored by China Academy of Launch Vehicle Technology.   It claims it is the only technical journal in China that comprehensively reports on both high-tech missiles and space launch vehicles.   The journal has the following major special columns: Expert Forum, Review and Commentary, Launch Vehicle Overall and Separation System Technologies, Research Paper and Technical Report, Research Briefing, Foreign Development, High-tech Window, and so on.

37. Guidance and Fuse

Zhidao yu Yinxin started publication in 1979 and is sponsored by CASC's 802 Institute.   It mainly covers papers dealing with missile systems, navigation guidance and detonation, airborne radar, short-distance radar, antennas, antenna blister, and so on.   The journal has the following major special columns: Navigation Guidance and Detonation Technology, Antenna Technology, Electronic Jamming Technology, Electronic Environmental Technology, Microwave Technology, Measurement Technology, Reliability Technology, Computer Technology, and so on.

Journal of Solid Rocket Technology

38. Guti Huojian Jishu started publication in 1979.   It is sponsored jointly by China Fourth Academy and the Solid Propulsion Committee of China Society of Astronautics.   It claims to be the only specialized journal in the world focused specifically on the solid rocket propulsion field.   The journal has the following major special columns: Engines, Propellant, Materials Processing, Measurement Technology,

and so on.   The Internet address of the journal is gthj.chinajournal.net.cn.

Spacecraft Recovery & Remote Sensing

39. Hangtian Fanhui yu Yaogan started publication in 1980.   It is sponsored by CASC's 508 Institute and introduces scientific accomplishments and developments in the areas of return spacecraft, manned space launch, space remote sensing, and so on, at home and abroad, to stimulate scientific research activities. The journal has the following major special columns: Space Return and Manned Spacecraft, Remote Sensing Technology, New Processes and Materials, Space Technology, and Space News Brief.

Chinese Journal of Aerospace Medicine

40. Zhongguo Hangtian Yiyao Zazhi started publication in 1999 and is sponsored by the general hospital of CASC.   It is a comprehensive medical journal covering both the most advanced development standards and the newest trends   in medical science in aerospace systems.   The journal has the following major special columns: Scientific Paper, Emergency Experience, Review, Lecture, Lesson, Technological Exchange, Clinic Pathological (Case) Discussion, R&D Trends at Home and Abroad, and so on.

Structure & Environment Engineering

41. Qiangdu yu Huanjing started publication in 1973 and is sponsored by CASC's 702 Institute.   The journal mainly covers engineering applications but also deals with theoretical analysis.   It has the following major special columns: Structural Strength, Fatigue, Rupture, Reliability, Reliability Engineering, Environment Engineering, Measurement, Disposal, Equipment, Measurement and Testing Technology, Engineering Management, and so on.

Aerospace Shanghai

42. Shanghai Hangtian, a bimonthly, started publication in 1984.   It is a comprehensive journal managed by the CASC and sponsored by the Shanghai Academy of Spaceflight Technology.   Issued both at home and abroad, the journal mainly carries academic and technical papers, research reports, technical reports, and special reviews that are related to satellite application, carrier rockets, and air defense missile systems and research, experiments, and applications for their subsystems.

Aerospace Techniques

43. Hangtian Gongyi, a bimonthly, is managed by CASC and sponsored by the Capital Aerospace Mechanical Co.   It is the only technical journal among the aerospace companies and organizations, mainly carrying scientific and technical papers and technological management articles on manufacturing technology for aerospace and civil products.   Its content covers welding, cold-heat-treatment processes, assembly techniques, and measuring technology.

CASIC Journals

Systems Engineering and Electronics

44. Xitong Gongcheng yu Dianzi Jishu started publication in 1979. It is managed by the China Aerospace Science and Industry Corporation (CASIC) and jointly sponsored by the 2nd Research Institute of CASIC,

the China Aerospace Society, and the China Systems Engineering Society.   It is a key, interdisciplinary journal that focuses on hi-tech development and application.   It aims to introduce new technology, promote academic exchange, and reflect the latest accomplishments in the two major areas of systems engineering and electronic technology.   The journal has special columns of Electronic Technology, Aerospace System Analysis, Defensive Electronic Technology, and so on.

Winged Missiles Journal

45. Feihang Daodan started publication in 1971.   It is managed by CASIC and sponsored by the 3rd Research Institute of CASIC.   It is a monthly journal of the 3rd Research Institute, mainly carrying research programs, developments, experiments, and practice of winged missiles in foreign countries and introducing various types of new technology, new materials, and new techniques in winged missiles development.   The journal aims to report in a timely fashion international news related to winged missiles and to boost winged missile programs to develop rapidly in China.   The journal has as main columns Missiles Survey, Information Exchange, Weapon System, Propulsion Technology, Control and Navigation Guidance, Unmanned Vehicle, and Process and Materials.

Aerospace Electronic Warfare

46. Hangtian Dianzi Duikang, a bimonthly, started publication in 1985; it is   managed by CASIC and sponsored by the 8511 Research Institute of CASIC.   It covers scientific and technological research, production, management, and teaching and learning in the field of electronic warfare and the research results and activity news of user companies and organizations.

Aeronautical Manufacturing Technology

47. Hangtian Zhizao Jishu started publication in 1983 and is sponsored by Beijing Aerospace Machinery Corporation.   It is a comprehensive technological journal covering various areas such as modern advanced manufacturing technology, new product R&D, product design innovation, technology management, production organization, and new aerospace manufacturing trends both at home and abroad in the development and manufacturing of the corresponding aeronautic and astronautic aircraft, manned spacecraft, and satellites.

Control Technology of Tactical Missiles

48. Zhanshu Daodan Kongzhi Jishu, a quarterly, started publication in 1980; it is managed by CASIC and sponsored by the Beijing Institute of Automatic Control Equipment.   As one of the key journals in China, it mainly covers autopilot-navigators, navigation guidance and control, accelerometers, and so on.

Journal of System Simulation

49. Xitong Fangzhen Xuebao started publication in 1989; it is managed by CASIC and sponsored by the China System Simulation Society.   It is a monthly academic journal of the Society.   The main contents of the journal are Analog Set Up and Simulation, Simulation Computers and Simulation Software, Simulation Devices in Training, Research and System Operations, Simulation Algorithms, Artificial Intelligence in Simulation, Simulation Technology of Concurrent Distribution and Interaction, and Analog Set Up and Simulation in Advanced Manufacturing.

Other Journals

Chinese Journal of Space Science

50. Kongjian Kexue Xuebao is jointly sponsored by the Center for Space Science and Applied Research of the Chinese Academy of Sciences and the China Space Science Society. It claims to be an influential and comprehensive publication focusing on space research accomplishments and basic research related to the space environment. The major branch disciplines covered in the journal include space astronomy, space physics, space chemistry, space geology, space life science, space materiel science, space earth science, and so on. The journal has main columns such as Theory and Research, Exploring and Experiment, Review and Briefing,

Remote Sensing Technology and Application

51. Yaogan Jishu yu Yingyong, a bimonthly, started publication in 1986 and is jointly sponsored by the Chinese Academy of Sciences Remote Sensing Joint Center and the Chinese Academy of Sciences Resources and Environmental Science Information Center. It is a comprehensive remote sensing academic journal mainly reporting new theories, new technology, new methods, new accomplishments, and development trends in the research and application of remote sensing technology at home and abroad. The journal has special columns of Research and Application, Development Trends, Geographic Information Systems, Image Processing, and Review,

Advanced Display

52. Xiandai Xianshi is a quarterly periodical on display technology. The Advanced Display Systems of U.S.A is its sponsor and financial supporter. It is also sponsored by the Beijing Research Institute of Telemetry. The content of the periodical covers the features, principles, structure, material, manufacturing techniques, applied technology, development trends, and marketplace of display technology. Its readers are engineers, teachers and students, and related government officials.

Spacecraft Engineering

53. Hangtianqi Gongcheng is a quarterly journal with strict restricted distribution. The main columns of the journal are Research and Design, Management and Practice, and Others.

Space Medicine & Medical Engineering

54. Hangtian Yixue yu Yixue Gongcheng, a bimonthly, started publication in 1988. It is jointly sponsored by the Headquarters Office of the PLA General Armament Department (GAD) and the Aerospace Medical Engineering Research Institute of the GAD. Issued at home and abroad, the journal mainly carries new theories, new accomplishments, new technology, and new trends in aeronautic and astronautic medicine, biological medical engineering, and research related to ergonomic engineering in China and foreign countries. Being one of the key journals in the areas of manned space flight and life science in China, it has special columns on Academic Books and Papers, Special Topic Commentary, Literature Review, Research Newsflash, News and Trends, and so on.

Chinese Journal of Aerospace Medicine

55. Zhonghua Hangkong Hangtian Yixue Zazhi, originally known as Zhonghua Hangkong Yixue Zazhi, started publication in 1990. It is sponsored by the Chinese Medical Association and published quarterly

in Chinese or English by the Press of the Chinese Journal of Aerospace Medicine.   The journal has special columns of Original Articles, Clinical Research, Review Articles, Aeromedical Practice, Case Reports, News and Notes, and so on.   Articles in this journal provide the latest available information on aviation medicine, space medicine, history of aerospace medicine, aerospace physiology, aerospace neurophysiology/vision, fatigue/circadian rhythms, acceleration/escape/impact, aerospace human factors, flight safety/accident investigation, performance/psychology/psychophysiology, air medical transport, hyperbaric medicine, and other related areas.   The journal aims to serve and support all those who explore, travel, work, or live in hazardous environments of aerospace.

Aerospace Medicine

56. Hangkong Hangtian Yiyao, a quarterly, started publication in 1990.   It is managed by the Office of Heilongjiang S&T for National Defense and sponsored by the Harbin 242 Hospital of China Aviation Industry Co.   The publication focuses on practical applicability and innovation.   The main columns of the journal are Experiment and Research, Aeronautic and Astronautic Medicine Clinical Books and Papers, Clinical Experience, Case Report, Prevention Medicine, Medical Information, and so on.

Experiments and Measurements in Fluid Mechanics

57. Liuti Lixue Shiyan yu Celiang, a quarterly, started publication in 1987 and is jointly sponsored by the China Aerodynamic Society and the China Aerodynamic Research and Development Center.   It is a state-level, comprehensive academic and technical publication with unrestricted distribution.   It is also a key journal on aviation and aerospace, mainly carrying new theories, new accomplishments, and new trends in fluid mechanics, especially in every aspect of testing and measurement of aerodynamics.

Acta Aerodynamica Sinica

58. Kongqi Donglixue Xuebao, a quarterly, started publication in 1980 and is jointly sponsored by the China Aerodynamic Society and the China Aerodynamic Research and Development Center.   It is a state-level, academic publication issued both at home and abroad.   As an important key journal in China, it mainly carries research papers and briefings on creative theory, experiment, and application in the field of aerodynamics.

Journal of Beijing University of Aeronautics and Astronautics

59. Beijing Hangkong Hangtian Daxue Xuebao, a monthly, started publication in 1956. It is managed by the Commission of Science, Technology, and Industry for National Defense and sponsored by the University.   It is a comprehensive academic journal focusing on aeronautic and astronautic science and technology.   The journal aims to introduce the University's R&D results and trends, promote academic exchange, educate creative professionals, and boost the transformation of R&D results into productive power.   It mainly carries research papers on material science and engineering, fluid mechanics and dynamic engineering, computer and application technology, and reliability and fault analysis in aeronautic and astronautic science and technology.

Journal of Nanjing University of Aeronautics & Astronautics

50. Nanjing Hangkong Hangtian Daxue Xuebao, a bimonthly, started publication in 1957.   It is managed by the Commission of Science, Technology, and Industry for National Defense and sponsored by the University.   It is a comprehensive academic journal reflecting scientific and technological

accomplishments in the areas of aeronautic and astronautic technology. It carries research papers, reviews, and ademic trend reports on dynamic engineering, automatic control, electronic engineering, manufacturing engineering, material science and technology, combustion theory, and so on.

Journal of Vibration Measurement & Diagnosis

61. Zhendong Ceshi yu Zhenduan, a quarterly, started publication in 1980. It is managed by the Commission of Science, Technology, and Industry for National Defense and jointly sponsored by the Universities Research Association of Mechanical Engineering Testing Technology and the Nanjing University of Aeronautics & Astronautics. It is a technical publication reflecting R&D results as well as the applications of these results in the areas of vibration, dynamic measurement, and fault diagnosis. The journal introduces domestic and international technical papers, special reports, and academic trends in the study and application of dynamic measurement theory, method, and approach, including testing technology, testing instruments development, system configuration, signal analysis, data processing, parametric recognition, and so on.

Journal of North China Institute of Astronautic Engineering

62. Huabei Hangtian Gongye Xueyuan Xuebao, a quarterly, started publication in 1989. It is managed by the Education Department of Hebei Province and sponsored by the Institute. It is a technical journal carrying academic papers and research reports in the areas of engineering technology application, natural science, social science, and so on.

Journal of National University of Defense Technology

63. Guofang Keji Daxue Xuebao, a bimonthly, started publication in 1956 and is sponsored by the University. Issued both at home and abroad, it is a comprehensive academic journal on engineering technology and natural science, reporting the latest R&D accomplishments and promoting academic exchange and personnel training. It mainly carries academic papers with ideas on innovation, reports on creative and practical technical accomplishments, reviews on important academic issues, and so on from within the University. It also includes and publishes those leading edge research papers from other universities based on projects sponsored by national and provincial funds.

Journal of Remote Sensing

64. Yaogan Xuebao, a bimonthly, started publication in 1997 and is sponsored by the Environmental Remote Sensing Association, the Geographical Society of China, and the Institute of Remote Sensing Application, Chinese Academy of Sciences. It is a professional academic journal reflecting scientific and technological research accomplishments and technical applications in the field of remote sensing, including these comprehensive application areas of aviation and aerospace, agricultural and forest resources development, geographic information systems, remote sensing, spatialization systems, and so on.

Journal of Projectiles, Rockets, Missiles, and Guidance

65. Danjian yu Zhidao Xuebao, a quarterly, started publication in 1980. It is managed by the China Association for Science and Technology and sponsored by the China Ordnance Society. The journal aims to publish academic papers on missiles, rockets, ammunition, guided weapons, and so on, highlighting new hi-tech accomplishments in this sector, introducing the latest application

accomplishments in scientific research, production, teaching-learning, and practice, and serving the modernization of China's national defense.

Journal of Vibration and Shock

66. Zhendong yu Chongji, a quarterly, started publication in 1982.   It is managed by the China Association for Science and Technology and jointly sponsored by the Chinese Society for Vibration Engineering, the Shanghai Jiaotong University, and the Shanghai Vibration Engineering Society.   It is a comprehensive, key academic journal introducing accomplishments and experience concerning vibration, ballistics, and noise in the fields of aviation, aerospace, shipbuilding, marine engineering, and environmental protection.   The content of the journal includes structural dynamic analysis, model analysis, parametric recognition, and so on.

Vacuum Electronics

67. Zhenkong Dianzi Jishu, a bimonthly, started publication in 1959.   It is managed by the Chinese Ministry of Information Industry and sponsored by the Beijing Institute of Vacuum Electronic Technology.   Issued at home and abroad, the journal is the only comprehensive technical publication in the field of vacuum electronic technology in China.   It is also the journal of the Vacuum Electronic Professional Society, mainly carrying articles on vacuum microwave devices, vacuum electronic devices, vacuum pumping, measurement and control, and so on.   The journal has special columns of Expert Forum, Research Report, Study and Design, New Technology Exchange, Techniques and Application, and Review.

Vacuum

68. Zhenkong, a bimonthly, started publication in 1994.   It is managed by the Chinese Ministry of Machine-Building Industry and sponsored by the Shengyang Institute of Vacuum Technology and the China Mechanized Equipment Group Co.   It is one of the major vacuum journals in China, with special columns on Expert Focus, Innovation Products, Solar Energy Utilization, Experience Exchange, Series of Lectures on Vacuum Technology and Application, and so on.

Vacuum Science and Technology

69. Zhenkong Kexue yu Jishu, a bimonthly, started publication in 1981.   It is managed by the China Association for Science and Technology and sponsored by the Chinese Vacuum Society.   It mainly covers vacuum technology, surface analysis, electronic materials, and so on.   The journal has special columns of Academic Papers, Summary Review, Technology Exchange, Scientific Research Trends, and so on.

Vacuum Communication

70. Zhenkong Tongxun, a bimonthly, started publication in 1973 and is jointly sponsored by the China General Mechanical Vacuum Equipment Association, the Mechanical Industry Vacuum S&T Information Net, the Zibo Vacuum Equipment Plant Co, Ltd, and Zhejiang Vacuum Equipment Group Co, Ltd.   The journal mainly covers practical problems in the application of vacuum technology and introduces development trends in this field.

Sichuan Vacuum

71. Sichuan Zhenkong, a semiannual, is jointly sponsored by the Sichuan Vacuum Society and the Guotou Nanguang Co, Ltd, introducing research accomplishments and development application of vacuum science and technology in Sichuan Province.

Shanghai Vacuum News

73. Shanghai Zhenkong Bao, a quarterly, started publication in 1990.   It is sponsored by the Shanghai Vacuum Society and Shanghai Five-Steel Special Metallurgy Co.   The paper aims to enhance the exchange between the Shanghai Vacuum Association and its members and to promote communication between the Association and vacuum circles at home and abroad.

Acta Materiae Compositae Sinica

74. Fuhe Cailiao Xuebao, a bimonthly, started publication in 1984 and is sponsored by the Chinese Complex Materials Society.   As an academic journal, it mainly carries scientific and technical papers and special reports written by well-known scientists and experts and reflects domestic and international innovative, high-level, significant research accomplishments and the latest research trends in complex materials' basic and application research.   The journal is of great reference value.

Journal of Engineering Thermophysics

75. Kongcheng Rewuli Xuebao, a bimonthly, started publication in 1980.   It is managed by the Chinese Academy of Sciences and jointly sponsored by the Chinese Engineering Thermophysics Society and the Engineering Thermophysics Institute of the Chinese Academy of Sciences.   It mainly carries scientific papers, research briefings, and important academic trends in engineering thermodynamics and power gear, theory of combustion, comprehensive utilization of energy, and so on.

Aerospace Materials and Technology

76. Yuhang Cailiao Gongyi started publication in 1971.   It is sponsored by the China Institute of Aerospace Materials and Processes and reports mainly scientific and technological advancements, R&D results, and engineering practice relating to aerospace materials and processes in China in the forms of scientific papers, research reports, review, and special discussion on new materials, new processes, and new products.   This journal was included in the list of China's one hundred key journals in the second national journal competition.

Journal of Astronautics

77. www.caaspace.org.cn/C_cbkw/C_cbkw.htm.

Yuhang Xuebao started publication in 1980.   It is sponsored by the China Society of Astronautics and reports research and development results in the field of aerospace in China, reflecting the hot, focal, and bright spots of China's aerospace research and development.   The journal has two main sections: Treatises and Research Notes.

Remote Sensing Information

78. Yaogan Xinxi, a quarterly, started publication in 1986.   It is managed by the Chinese State Bureau of

Surveying and Mapping (CSBSM) and sponsored by the National S&T Department Remote Sensing Center of the CSBSM.   The main columns of the journal include Forum, Theory and Study, Application Technology, Scientific Accomplishments, Translated Text, International Trend, Knowledge Window, and Remote Sensing Technical Equipment.

Journal of Flight Vehicle Measurement and Control

79. Feixingqi Cekong Xuebao, a quarterly, started publication in 1982 and issponsored by the Beijing Institute of Tracking and Communication Technology.   The journal won the third S&T Progress Award conferred by the Commission of Science, Technology, and Industry for National Defense in 1986, received the third Military S&T Journal Award in 1991, and won the title of "Excellent National Defense S&T Journal" in 1996.   Its main columns include General Measurement and Control, Data Processing, Radio Measurement and Control, Computer Technology, GPS Application, Newsflash, and so on.

Journal of Science Technology and Industry for National Defense

80. Guofang Keji Gongye, a monthly publication issued both at home and abroad, is sponsored by the Commission of Science, Technology, and Industry for National Defense.   It is the only journal that reports news for the overall national defense science and technology industry in China.   Integrating guidance, academics, comprehensiveness, and expertise, it is an authoritative publication covering China's nuclear technology, aerospace, aviation, shipbuilding, weapons, military electronics, and other related industries.

References Professor Liu Huanyu of Dalian Naval Academy: "Sea-Based Anti-Satellite Platform"45

[1] Jiang Panling, et al, The threat of electronic attack on military space systems, Electronic Countermeasure in Space, 2003 (1).

[2] Kang Feng, Status and development trend of space intelligence warfare in the United States, Foreign Electronic War, 2003, (1).

[3] Wang Haisheng, Analysis of the United States star war, Foreign Electronic War, 2003, (1).

[4] Li Dongyuan, Introduction to ground-based anti-satellite electro-optical detection system in foreign nations, Electro-optical Countermeasure and Passive Interference, 2003, (1)

[5] Wang Jianxun, et al, Feasibility analysis of electronic jamming of military satellites, Radar and Countermeasure, 2003, (1).

[6] Ren Ning, et al, Introduction to foreign laser countermeasure early warning satellite, Electro-optical Countermeasure and Passive Interference, 2003, (1).

[7] Pu Lingke, Laser weapons and defense technology, Electronic Engineering News, 2003, (1).

---

45 Jianchuan Kexue Jishu, Feb 2004.

[8] Zhang Jie, Laser threat caused by military laser technology development, intelligence command control system and authentication technology, 2003, (3).

[9] Wang Jingrui, Development and military applications of electromagnetic launching technology, Fire Power and Command Control, 2001, (1).

[10] Wang Yandong, Kinetic energy anti-satellite weapons in the United States, Defense Technology Foundation, 2003 (3).

[11] Jin Shichuan and Xia Wencheng, War-fighting capability and characteristics of electronic information hardware in the united States, Foreign Electronic War, 2003, (1).

[12] Yuan Jun, Introduction to anti-satellite weapons development in the United States, Satellite Application, 2001, (12)

[13] Chen Yourong, et al, Star wars will be difficult to avoid in the 21st century, Satellite Application, 2001, (12).

[14] Yang Juan, Military space and national security, Satellite Application, 2001, (9).

[15] Chen Kaoliang, Development trend in the united States Space System, Satellite Application, 2001, (6).

[16] Huang Zhicheng, Anti-satellite weapons and space military control, Satellite Application, 2000, (9).

[17] Institute of Space Technology and Information, National Space Security Evaluation Report, Satellite Application, 2001, (6), 2001, (9), 2001(12).

[18] tan Xianyu, Status and development of GPS countermeasure technology, Modern Defense Technology, 2003, (1).

[19] Tong Shengkui, Ocean Reconnaissance Satellite Project of the Soviet Union, Satellite Application, 2000, (9).

[20] Shen Chengzhong, Position and role of remote sensing satellite in modern high tech local war, Satellite Application, 2000, (9).

References to ASAT vs. Space Defense Weapons [2005] [46]

(1) Du Rongsun: Anti-satellite and satellite defense [J], Spacecraft Engineering, 1992(2).

(2) Liu Shaoqiu, Gao Shuxia, Gao Yonghao, et al: Analysis of R&D status of anti-satellite weapons [J], Journal of Systems Engineering and Electronics, 1994.

---

[46] Zhanshu Daodan Kongzhi Jishu 01 Dec 05;Wang Wenfeng, Yang Jianjun and Huang Xueyu: (Missile Institute, the Air Force Engineering University, Sanyuan, Shaaxi "A Campaign Efficiency Evaluation Model of Anti-Satellite Weapon "; Wang Wenfeng (1980-) is a Master's degree student with the Missile Institute, the Air Force Engineering University.

(3) Cheng Chuanhao, Wang Ruichen and Lu Dexin: Penetration and interception of ballistic missiles [J], Modern Defence Technology, April 2002, 30(2).

(4) Heang Zuwei: Military Satellite Systems and Anti-satellite Anti-missile Technology, AD-D300518.

(5) Gan Yingai et al (edited): Operations research [M], Tsinghua University Press, 1990.

Bibliography on Space Arms Control

Logsdon, John M., 2001, Just Say Wait to Space Power, *Issues in Science and Technology*, vol. 17, no. 3 (spring), p. 33. Argues that the United States should not pursue space control and weaponization before undertaking broad public discussions. http://www.nap.edu/issues/17.3/p_logsdon.htm

Moltz, James Clay (ed.), 2002, *Future Security in Space: Commercial, Military and Arms Control Tradeoffs,* The Center for Nonproliferation Studies at the Monterey Institute of International Studies (Occasional Paper no. 10). Contains articles concerning background issues, alternatives and proposals on space security. http://cns.miis.edu./pubs/opapers/op10/op10.pdf

Moore, Mike, 2001, Watch out for Space Command, *Bulletin of the Atomic Scientists,* vol. 57, no. 1(January), pp. 24–25. Warns that the United States Space Command is intent on militarily dominating space with space-based weapons, despite the push from the international community to outlaw weapons in space. http://www.thebulletin.org/issues/2001/jf01/jf01mmoore.html

——, 2001, Non-aggressive Weapons?, *Bulletin of the Atomic Scientists,* vol. 57, no. 2 (March), pp. 17–19. Summarizes the Space Commission Report and examines its underlying implications for the development of space-based weapons. http://www.thebulletin.org/issues/2001/ma01/ma01rmoore.html

Preston, Bob, et al., 2002, *Space Weapons Earth Wars*, Project Air Force, RAND. Describes space weapons, acquisition methods, threat perceptions and possible responses. http://www.rand.org/publications/MR/MR1209/

Saperstein, Al, 2002, Weaponization vs. Militarization of Space, *Physics and Society,* vol. 31, no. 3 (July). Underscores the differences between the weaponization and militarization of space. Includes discussion on how space could be weaponized by certain states in the future. http://www.aps.org/units/fps/jul02/index.html

Union of Concerned Scientists, 2002, *Limitations and Artificialities of the Testing Program*. Interactive demonstration of the missile defence tests of the United States and explains how the tests have failed to demonstrate that such a system will be successful in an actual attack. http://www.ucsusa.org/global_security/missile_defense/page.cfm?pageID=1026

Bunn, George and John B. Rhinelander, 2002, Outer Space Treaty May Ban Strike Weapons, *Arms Control Today,* vol. 32, no. 5 (June), p. 24. Argues that the Outer Space Treaty already addresses the stationing of strike weapons in LEO. http://www.armscontrol.org/act/2002_06/letterjune02.asp

DeBlois, Bruce M., 1998, Space Sanctuary: A Viable National Strategy, *Airpower Journal*, vol. 12, no. 4 (winter). Comprehensive article addressing the various aspects of the weaponization of space, including political and financial concerns, threat potentials, and technological limitations. Argues for the preservation of space as a peaceful medium. http://www.airpower.maxwell.af.mil/airchronicles/apj/apj98/win98/deblois.html

Garwin, Richard L., 1999, *Toward International Security: The Development of Space Weapons, ASAT Testing, and National Missile Defense*. Advocates international discussion on the ban of weapons in space and ASAT testing. http://www.fas.org/rlg/102599-lakhdhir.htm one • 2003 69

Johnson, Rebecca, 2001, Multilateral Approaches to Preventing the Weaponisation of Space, *Disarmament Diplomacy*, Issue 56 (April). Proposes that an independent conference be convened to negotiate a new multilateral treaty on the prohibition of space-based weapons. http://www.acronym.org.uk/dd/dd56/56rej.htm

Moltz, James Clay, 2002, Breaking the Deadlock on Space Arms Control, *Arms Control Today,* vol. 32, no. 3 (April). Reviews the history of the space weapons debate and offers a compromise proposal. http://www.armscontrol.org/act/2002_04/moltzapril02.asp

Proposed Treaty on the Limitation of the Military Use of Outer Space, 1984. Proposal to ban all forms of space-based weapons. http://www.mbmd.org/SpaceWeaponsBan/GoettingenTreaty.pdf

Space Preservation Act of 2002, HR 3616, January 2002. Bill introduced to the United States House of Representatives in order to prohibit the weaponization of space. http://www.pnnd.org/us_space_preservation_bill.htm

White, Robert E., 2001, *Preserving Space for Peaceful Use: A Case for a New Space Treaty*, Auckland, New Zealand, Centre for Peace Studies (Working Paper no. 10). Argues against the development of weapons in space, including an outline for a new treaty banning the weaponization of outer space. http://www.converge.org.nz/pma/sptreaty.doc

Working Paper Presented by the Delegations of China, the Russian Federation, Viet Nam, Indonesia, Belarus, Zimbabwe and Syria: Possible Elements for a Future International Legal Agreement on the Prevention of the Deployment of Weapons in Outer Space, the Threat or Use of Force Against Outer Space Objects (Russia-China CD Working Paper). Paper submitted to the Conference on Disarmament on 27 June 2002. http://www.acronym.org.uk/docs/0206/doc10.htm

Federation of American Scientists, World Space Guide. See <http://www.fas.org/spp/guide/index.html>.

Contant, Corine and Lawrence Cooper, 2000, The People's Republic of China: Consolidating its Space Power, Enhancing its Military Might, in Rebecca Jimerson and Ray A. Williamson (eds.), *Space and Military Power in East Asia,* Washington DC, George Washington University, Space Policy Institute. Assesses China's military space power and technological developments, as well as the potential implications for the United States. http://www.gwu.edu/~spi/spacemilch1.html

Gauthier, Katheryn, 1999, *China as Peer Competitor?,* Air University Research Papers. Presents evidence suggesting that China has the potential to become a competitor of the United States as the margin of military advantages between these two states in information warfare, weaponry and space

technology are declining.
http://www.iwar.org.uk/iwar/resources/usaf/maxwell/students/1999/max18.htm

Jimerson, Rebecca, 2000, North Korea: Locked in a Space Race with the World, in Rebecca Jimerson and Ray A. Williamson (eds.), *Space and Military Power in East Asia,* Washington DC, George Washington University, Space Policy Institute.

The Airborne Laser Narrows Its Beam
By John A. Tirpak, Executive Editor

The Airborne Laser, formerly a full-up weapon development project, was recently reduced to a basic technology demonstration effort. Some thought the demotion was a prelude to harsher action and that the Pentagon soon would kill off the program altogether.

It hasn't turned out that way. In fact, the program, though long delayed, is far from dead. Its managers still aim to deliver a critical fighting capability to the nation.

The effort has been narrowed considerably, though. The ABL project is today focused on a single goal: demonstrating that the system can shoot down a ballistic missile in its boost phase. Nearly all planning and engineering aimed at future operational versions of the system has been put on hold, pending the success of a real-world test set for late 2008.

The Air Force envisioned a fleet of seven ABLs, which it saw as the minimum needed to maintain one "orbit"—a 24/7 capability—in a given regional hot spot.

However, the program has been beset by chronic delays. Target shootdown dates slipped several times, and the new 2008 goal is more than six years past the originally planned lethal test in 2002.

Reason for Optimism

Still, many are upbeat. In April, Obering told the Senate Armed Services Committee strategic forces panel that, even though there are "many technical challenges with the Airborne Laser," the run of successes since 2004 "gives me reason to be optimistic that we can produce an effective directed energy capability. An operational Airborne Laser could provide a valuable boost-phase defense capability against missiles of all ranges."

The "down payment" on the second airplane—funding for long-lead production parts—is not now scheduled until Fiscal 2011. Modifications to an airframe probably wouldn't start until 2013, "so, realistically, ... we wouldn't be back in the air with a second airplane, doing testing with the weapon system, before the 2015-2016 timeframe," Daniels forecast.

June 2006, Vol. 89, No. 6

Toward A New Laser Era
By Hampton Stephens

The ABL, however, probably will mark just the start of a broader laser era. Service officials believe the combat potential of lasers—for offensive and defensive weapons, protective systems, sensors, and myriad other military applications—goes well beyond the multibillion-dollar ABL program itself. (See "Attack at the Speed of Light," December 2002, p. 26.) Those capabilities include attack at light speed, dead-on accuracies, and uncompromised lethality, according to Col. Gail Wojtowicz, chief of the Future Concepts and Transformation Division in the Office of the Deputy Chief of Staff for Plans and Programs.

Master Plan

To prepare, the future concepts division recently completed work on an Air Force directed energy master plan that examines how lasers and other directed energy technologies could be integrated with Air Force platforms. The master plan was ordered after a 2004 wargame demonstrated the battlefield potential of a number of directed energy capabilities, said Wojtowicz. Potential directed energy capabilities, including lasers, were a focus in the follow-on Future Capabilities Assessment '05 wargame, held last October.

Laser Gunships?

Another capability the Air Force would like to see developed quickly is an aircraft-mounted tactical laser. Since 2001, US Special Operations Command has sponsored an Advanced Tactical Laser concept demonstration. Such a system, if it proved out, could eventually be mounted on an AC-130 Gunship for use against ground targets.

The bottom line is that there is no simple solution to guarantee beam control. Though AFRL is making progress on all technological fronts, Hamil predicts it will be at least 10 years "and probably 20 years" before solid-state laser weapons are flying around, usable in combat.

"I would suggest to you that in the long term, 15 years plus, directed energy [will have] the greatest transformational effect on how we fight wars," Wojtowicz said.

While Wojtowicz's office is attempting to see what the future holds for directed energy, the service's Directed Energy Task Force is making sure the Air Force is preparing for that future. Headed by Maj. Gen. Stanley Gorenc, director of operational capability requirements, the task force is looking across all Air Force functions—doctrine, organization, training, materiel, leadership, personnel, and facilities—to make sure directed energy is being considered.

Defenses against directed energy capabilities are a special concern of the task force, because US enemies are known to be pursuing such technology. That's one reason the Air Force Secretary and Chief of Staff decided to establish the task force, even before requirements for DE-related capabilities existed in many cases.

US Aerospace Research and Development Funding Trends[47]

Aerospace R&D includes a wide range of activities, from basic scientific research to the development of new technologies in increasingly diverse fields of study. Federal dollars continue to be a significant contributor to U.S. aerospace R&D, but in recent years, the federal role has declined relative to industry funding. The three major federal agencies that support aerospace R&D— Defense, NASA, and FAA—have different priorities and missions that are reflected in their respective R&D portfolios. Defense's R&D budget is greater than any other agency—with a large majority of its R&D funds supporting development projects—and its R&D budgets for air and space R&D has increased in recent years. NASA's current prioritization of space exploration has driven R&D funding priorities, and under current plans NASA will provide more funding for development activities than for basic and applied research. Likewise, NASA's projected funding for aeronautics research and science is in slight decline. FAA, with the smallest R&D budget of the three agencies, focuses funding on the development of the next generation air transportation system (NGATS), but its R&D funding has also declined.

Aerospace R&D includes a wide range of activities such as basic research, applied research, and development. Basic research works to expand fundamental knowledge in areas such as physics, chemistry, and mathematics without specific applications in mind; however, it may include activities with broad applications. Applied research aims to gain knowledge applicable to solving specific and identified needs, building on the general work of the basic sciences. Applied aerospace research includes activities to develop better propulsion and power technology, advanced spacecraft technology, and crew and personnel protection technology. Development projects use the knowledge and understanding developed by researchers to build new, or improve existing, systems. New military weapons systems, a replacement for the space shuttle, and new commercial aircraft are all examples of major development projects.

Increasingly, R&D in areas not traditionally associated with aerospace, such as computer software, has applicability to the sector. At the same time, long-established areas for aerospace research may bring benefits to other economic sectors. For example, advances in software might benefit new flight control systems and have applications to banking, or new ceramic materials developed for airplanes might be used in automobiles. Researchers do not always know beforehand where the results of their work will find useful applications

The federal government's support of R&D has been critical to maintaining the nation's global leadership in the aerospace industry. For example, government-supported research enabled the development of jet engine technologies that helped U.S. commercial and military aircraft manufacturers achieve global prominence. According to industry statistics, aerospace companies are funding an increasing portion of industrial R&D than they did in the past.[1] In fiscal year 2003, the most recent year for which data are available, federal funds supported
48 percent of industry R&D in the aerospace industry, whereas in 1999 the federal share was 63 percent. Nevertheless, the federal role remains significant.

---

[47] Source: GAO Report to the Ranking Democratic Member, Subcommittee on Aviation, Committee on Transportation and Infrastructure, House of Representatives, "U.S. AEROSPACE INDUSTRY Progress in Implementing Aerospace Commission Recommendations, and Remaining Challenges" September 2006, GAO-06-920.

Industrial R&D tends to focus on technology development that is specific to individual company products. As a result, company funding is significantly lower for basic and applied research than for development. According to aerospace industry statistics, federal dollars fund the majority of the basic and applied research performed by the aerospace industry, whereas most development is funded by companies themselves. In dollar terms, development expenditures, by both companies and the federal government, are much higher than research expenditures. Nonetheless, federal funds provide the dominant share of applied research support, in particular. Aerospace industry experts told us that, if industry is to benefit from federally funded basic and applied research, new technologies must be developed to a relatively high level to be easily applied to product development. Likewise, our prior work has found that technologies with a high level of maturity are more likely to be applied successfully to product development projects. An individual company is unlikely to invest its own money in basic and applied research that offers uncertain payoffs and might benefit competitors. Like Defense's budget in general, Defense's overall R&D budget has increased in recent years and is the largest federal supporter of R&D.[2] Its current modernization effort is driving increases in R&D expenditures for developing major weapons systems, including aviation, missile, and space systems. In 2005, with a budget of $8.1 billion, the ballistic missile defense program was the largest R&D program in Defense—nearly more than twice the budget of the Joint Strike Fighter, the second largest program. The Aeronautics and Space Report of the President estimates Defense's budget for space activities in fiscal year 2006 at $22.7 billion—over $7 billion more than NASA's. Within Defense's R&D budget are funds for science and technology activities. These fund R&D that is typically not associated with specific weapons systems and potentially can benefit a wide range of military and civilian applications.[3] Since 2001, Defense's science and technology budget has increased for both air and space activities.For the purposes of this report, Defense's Research, Development, Testing and Evaluation budget is referred to as Defense's R&D budget.[3]Defense's R&D budget is divided into seven categories in the Defense budget: basic research, applied research, advanced technology development, demonstration and validation, engineering and manufacturing development, management support, and operational systems development. The first three categories are referred to as science and technology.

Figure 7: Defense Budget for Science and Technology for Air and Space Platforms, Fiscal Years 2001-2005

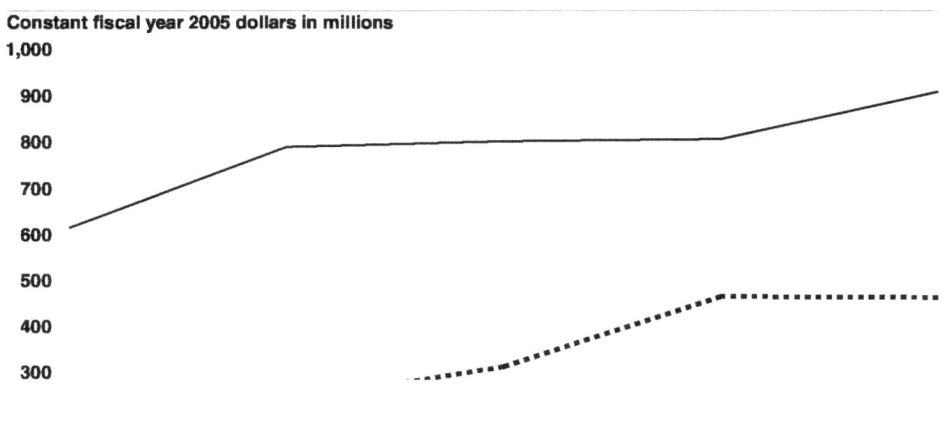

200

100

0

2001   2002

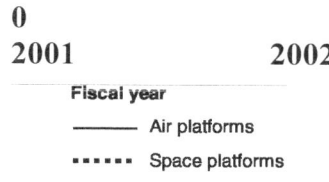

Fiscal year
——— Air platforms
· · · · · · Space platforms
Source: GAO analysis of Defense data.

Note: Fiscal year 2005 is the latest year for which these data are available.

Figure 8: Defense Budget Authority for Basic and Applied Research, and for Development, Fiscal Years 1999–2007

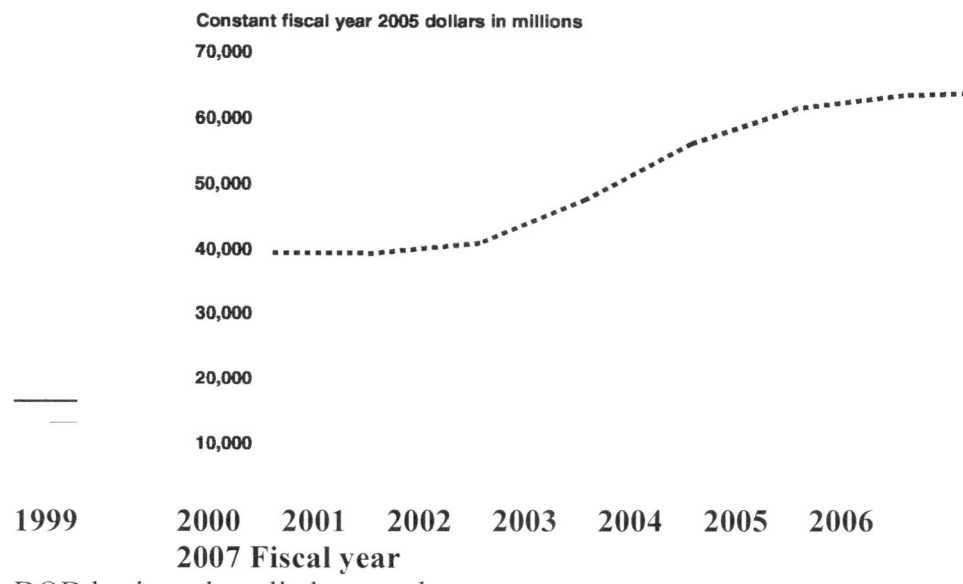

Constant fiscal year 2005 dollars in millions

70,000

60,000

50,000

40,000

30,000

20,000

10,000

1999   2000   2001   2002   2003   2004   2005   2006
            2007 Fiscal year

DOD basic and applied research

DOD development

Source: GAO analysis of Defense budget documents.

Note: Defense funding data are not specific to aerospace activities. Fiscal year 2007 data come from the President's proposed budget; 2006 data are estimated outlays.

NASA's R&D includes a broad range of complex and technical activities—from space exploration to scientific observations of the solar system to the development of new aviation technologies, including those needed for NGATS. According to the President's proposed fiscal year 2007 budget and NASA's current plans, space exploration activities, including R&D, will continue to be the largest part of NASA's budget in the future. This trend will be driven by the development of a replacement vehicle for the space shuttle, manned lunar exploration, and robotic and manned Mars exploration missions. In contrast, funding for aeronautics research and some space and earth science research within NASA will decline until fiscal year

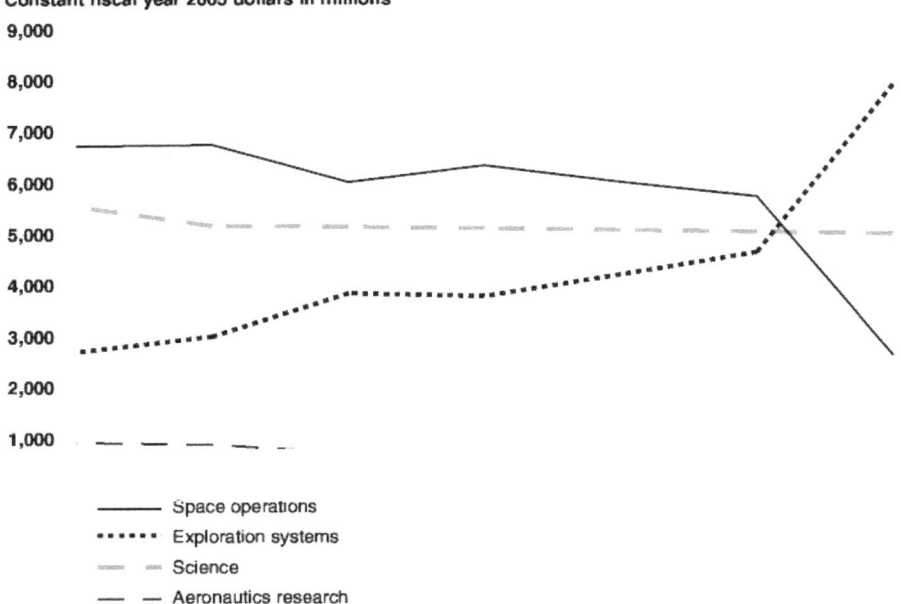

Constant fiscal year 2005 dollars in millions

——— Space operations
•••••• Exploration systems
═══ ═══ Science
— — Aeronautics research

Source: GAO analysis of the President's fiscal year 2007 budget request for NASA.

Notes: Space operations includes the space shuttle, International Space Station, and flight support. Exploration systems includes the budgets for developing new space vehicles, such as the Crew Launch Vehicle and Crew Exploration Vehicle. Science includes earth-sun, solar system, and universe programs. Aeronautics research is the total budget for the Aeronautics Research Mission Directorate.

Fiscal year 2005 and fiscal year 2006 are actual funding amounts.

Like NASA's budget overall, the agency's R&D funding is relatively stable, but current space exploration plans call for a shift toward more development and less research. Consequently, NASA's funding for basic and applied research ——— has been declining while its funding for development has increased (see fig. 10).

Figure 10: NASA's Budget Authority for Basic and Applied Research, and for Development, Fiscal Years 1999–2007

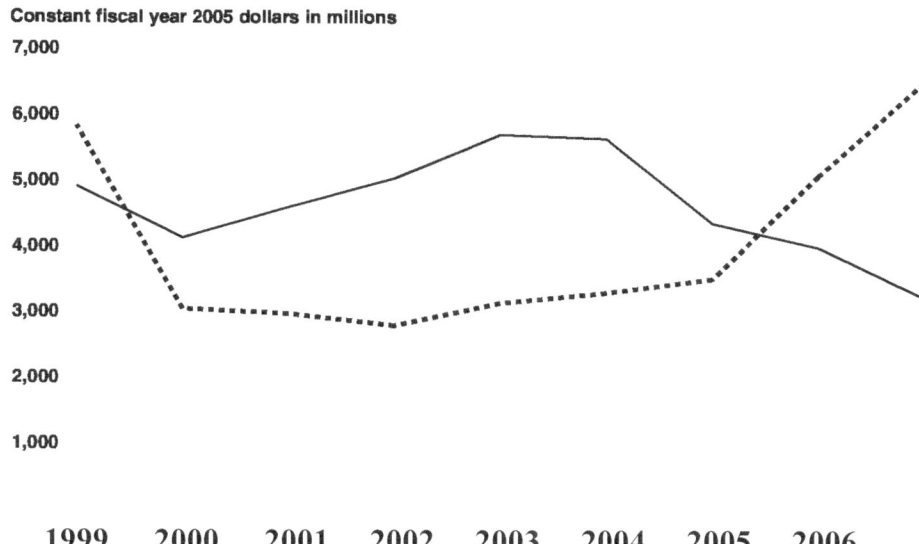

Constant fiscal year 2005 dollars in millions

7,000

6,000

5,000

4,000

3,000

2,000

1,000

1999   2000   2001   2002   2003   2004   2005   2006
2007 Fiscal year

NASA basic and applied research NASA development
Source: GAO analysis of budget documents.

www.ingramcontent.com/pod-product-compliance
Lightning Source LLC
Chambersburg PA
CBHW082146290526
45794CB00008B/3179